Celtic Language Technology Workshop 2019

Held at Machine Translation Summit XVII

Dublin, Ireland
19 August 2019

ISBN: 978-1-5108-9247-7

Printed from e-media with permission by:

Curran Associates, Inc.
57 Morehouse Lane
Red Hook, NY 12571

Some format issues inherent in the e-media version may also appear in this print version.

Copyright© (2019) by the Association for Computational Linguistics
All rights reserved.
Copyright for individual papers remains with the authors and are licensed under a Creative Commons 4.0
license, CC-BY-ND. (https://creativecommons.org/licenses/by-nd/4.0/)

Printed by Curran Associates, Inc. (2019)

For permission requests, please contact the Association for Computational Linguistics
at the address below.

Association for Computational Linguistics
209 N. Eighth Street
Stroudsburg, Pennsylvania 18360

Phone: 1-570-476-8006
Fax: 1-570-476-0860

acl@aclweb.org

Additional copies of this publication are available from:

Curran Associates, Inc.
57 Morehouse Lane
Red Hook, NY 12571 USA
Phone: 845-758-0400
Fax: 845-758-2633
Email: curran@proceedings.com
Web: www.proceedings.com

Machine Translation Summit XVII

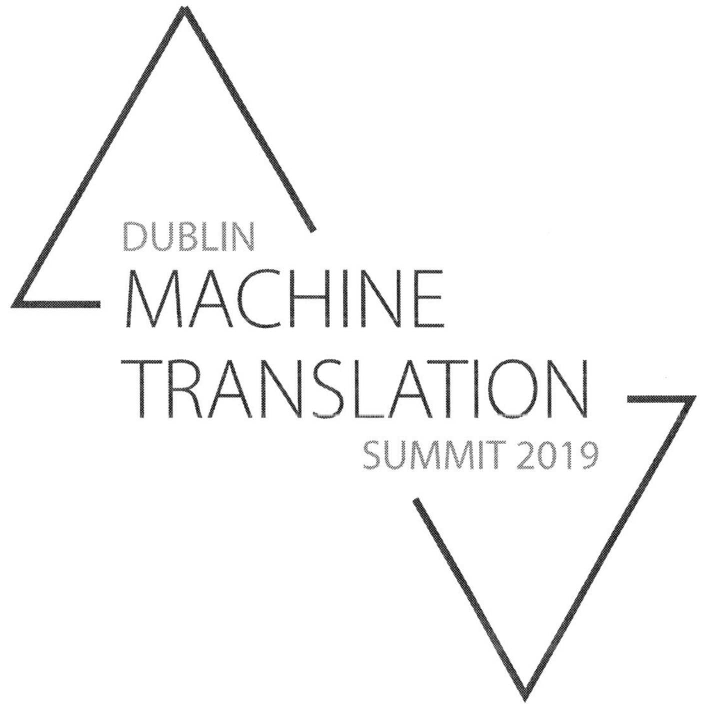

Proceedings of the Celtic Language Technology Workshop 2019

http://cl.indiana.edu/cltw19/

19th August, 2019
Dublin, Ircland

© 2019 The authors. These articles are licensed under a Creative Commons 4.0 licence, no derivative works, attribution, CC-BY-ND.

Proceedings of the Celtic Language Technology Workshop 2019

http://cl.indiana.edu/cltw19/

19th August, 2019
Dublin, Ireland

Preface from the co-chairs of the workshop

These proceedings include the program and papers presented at the third Celtic Language Technology Workshop held in conjunction with the Machine Translation Summit in Dublin in August 2019. Celtic Languages are spoken in regions extending from the British Isles to the western seaboard of continental Europe, and communities in Argentina and Canada. They include Irish, Scottish Gaelic, Breton, Manx, Welsh and Cornish. Irish is an official EU language, both Irish and Welsh have official language status in their respective countries, and Scottish Gaelic recently saw an improvement in its prospects through the Gaelic Language (Scotland) Act 2005. The majority of others have co-official status, except Breton which has not yet received recognition as an official or regional language.

Until recently, the Celtic languages have lagged behind in the area of natural language processing (NLP) and machine translation (MT). Consequently, language technology research and resource provision for this language group was poor. In recent years, as the resource provision for minority and under-resourced languages has been improving, it has been extended and applied to some Celtic languages.. The CLTW community and workshop, inaugurated at COLING (Dublin) in 2014, provides such a forum for researchers interested in language/speech processing technologies and related resources for low-resourced languages, specifically those working with the Celtic languages.

The 11 accepted papers cover an extremely wide range of topics, including machine translation, treebanking, computer-aided language learning, NLP of social media, information retrieval, Old Irish, the Welsh spoken in Argentina and named entity recognition.

We thank our invited speakers, Claudia Soria of the National Research Council of Italy and Kelly Davis of Mozilla. Claudia studies digital language diversity and Kelly is part of Mozilla's open-source Common Voice speech project. We also thank our authors and presenters for their hard work and workshop attendees for their participation, and of course we are very grateful to our programme committee for reviewing and providing invaluable feedback on the work published. Finally we thank Mozilla and the Department of Culture, Heritage and the Gaeltacht for financial support.

Workshop organisers

Teresa Lynn, Dublin City University
Delyth Prys, University of Bangor
Colin Batchelor, Royal Society of Chemistry
Francis M. Tyers, Indiana University and Higher School of Economics

Organisers

Workshop chairs

Teresa Lynn	Dublin City University
Delyth Prys	University of Bangor
Colin Batchelor	Royal Society of Chemistry
Francis M. Tyers	Indiana University, Higher School of Economics

Programme committee

Andrew Carnie	University of Arizona
Annie Foret	Université Rennes 1
Arantza Diaz de Ilarraza	Euskal Herriko Unibertsitatea
Brian Davis	Maynooth University
Brian Ó Raghallaigh	Fiontar/Dublin City University
Elaine Uí Dhonnchadha	Trinity College Dublin
Jeremy Evas	Cardiff University and Welsh Government
John Judge	ADAPT Centre, Dublin City University
John McCrae	INSIGHT Centre, University of Galway
Kepa Sarasola	Euskal Herriko Unibertsitatea
Kevin Scannell	St. Louis University
Mikel L. Forcada	Universitat d'Alacant
Monica Ward	Dublin City University
Montse Maritxalar	Euskal Herriko Unibertsitatea
Nancy Stenson	University College Dublin
Pauline Welby	CNRS/University College Dublin
William Lamb	University of Edinburgh

Contents

Unsupervised Multi–Word Term Recognition in Welsh

Irena Spasić
School of Computer Science & Informatics
Cardiff University
SpasicI@cardiff.ac.uk

David Owen
School of Computer Science & Informatics
Cardiff University
OwenDW1@cardiff.ac.uk

Dawn Knight
School of English, Communication & Philosophy
Cardiff University
KnightD5@cardiff.ac.uk

Andreas Artemiou
School of Mathematics
Cardiff University
ArtemiouA@cardiff.ac.uk

Abstract

This paper investigates an adaptation of an existing system for multi-word term recognition, originally developed for English, for Welsh. We overview the modifications required with a special focus on an important difference between the two representatives of two language families, Germanic and Celtic, which is concerned with the directionality of noun phrases. We successfully modelled these differences by means of lexico–syntactic patterns, which represent parameters of the system and, therefore, required no re–implementation of the core algorithm. The performance of the Welsh version was compared against that of the English version. For this purpose, we assembled three parallel domain–specific corpora. The results were compared in terms of precision and recall. Comparable performance was achieved across the three domains in terms of the two measures (P = 68.9%, R = 55.7%), but also in the ranking of automatically extracted terms measured by weighted kappa coefficient (κ = 0.7758). These early results indicate that our approach to term recognition can provide a basis for machine translation of multi-word terms.

1 Introduction

Terms are noun phrases (Daille, 1996; Kageura, 1996) that are frequently used in specialised texts to refer to concepts specific to a given domain (Arppe, 1995). In other words, terms are linguistic representations of domain-specific concepts (Frantzi, 1997). As such, terms are key means of communicating effectively in a scientific or technical discourse (Jacquemin, 2001). To ensure that terms conform to specific standards, they often undergo a process of standardisation. Such standards are commonly based on the following principles. First and foremost, a term should be linguistically correct and reflect the key characteristics of the concept it represents in concise manner. There should only be one term per concept and all other variations (e.g. acronyms and inflected forms) should be derivatives of that term. TermCymru, a terminology used by the Welsh Government translators, assigns a status to each term depending on the degree to which it has been standardised: fully standardised, partially standardised and linguistically verified.

Terms will still naturally vary in length and their level of fixedness, i.e. the strength of association between specific lexical items (Nattinger and DeCarrico, 1992), which can be measured using mutual information, z-score or t-score. Such variation of terms within a language may pose problems when attempting to translate term variants consistently into another language. Verbatim translations also often deviate from the established terminology in the target language, e.g. TermCymru in Welsh. Therefore, high-quality translations, performed by either humans or machines, require management of terminologies. Specialised text requires consistent use of terminology, where the same term is used consistently throughout a discourse to refer to the same concept. Very often, terms cannot be translated word for word. Therefore, most machine translation systems maintain a term base in order to support translations that use established terminology in the target language.

Given a potentially unlimited number of domains as well as a dynamic nature of many domains (e.g. computer science) where new terms get introduced regularly, manual maintenance of one-to-one term bases for each pair of languages may become unmanageable. Where parallel corpora exist, automatic term recognition approaches can be used to extract terms and their translations, which can then be embedded into the term base to support machine translation of other document from the same domain. To that end, we are focusing on comparing the performance of an unsupervised approach to automatic term recognition in two languages, Welsh and English, as an important step towards machine translation of specialised texts in the given languages.

2 Methods

2.1 Method overview

FlexiTerm is a software tool that automatically identifies multi-word terms (MWTs) in text documents (Spasić et al., 2013). Given a domain-specific corpus of plain text documents, it will extract MWTs in a form of a lexicon, which links together different forms of the same term including acronyms (Spasić, 2018). The most recent version can arrange the lexicon hierarchically (Spasić et al., 2018). Table 1 provides examples of terms that were automatically extracted from patent applications from three different domains.

Domain	Term variants
Civil engineering	bottom hole assembly bottomhole assembly BHA
Computing	network functions virtualization NFV virtual network function VNF
Transport	lightning strike protection LSP protection against lightning strike

Table 1: Examples of domain-specific terms

FlexiTerm performs MWT recognition in two stages. First, MWT candidates are selected using lexico-syntactic patterns. This is based on an assumption that terms follow certain formation patterns (Justeson & Katz, 1995). Indeed, terms are associated with preferred phrase structures. They are typically noun phrases that consist of adjectives, nouns and prepositions. Terms rarely contain verbs, adverbs or conjunctions.

Once potential MWT are identified, they are ranked using a measure that combines their length and frequency with an aim of identifying the longest repetitive patterns of word usage. This is based on an assumption that MWTs are expected to demonstrate collocational stability (Smadja, 1993).

The original FlexiTerm method was implemented to support the English language. In the following sections, we describe the modifications that were required to support the same functionality in the Welsh language.

2.2 Linguistic pre-processing

FlexiTerm takes advantage of lexico–syntactic information to identify term candidates. Therefore, the input documents need to undergo linguistic pre–

processing in order to annotate them with relevant lexico–syntactic information. This process includes part-of-speech (POS) tagging, sentence splitting and tokenisation. The original implementation of FlexiTerm uses Stanford CoreNLP library (Toutanova et al., 2003) to support such processing in English. In the Welsh version, text is processed using the Canolfan Bedwyr Welsh POS Tagger (Jones, Robertson, and Prys, 2015) to tokenise the text and tag each token with an appropriate lexical category including end-of-sentence annotations. A subset of relevant tags from Canolfan Bedwyr Welsh language tag set (Robertson, 2015) were mapped to tags compatible with the original version of FlexiTerm to minimise re-implementation (e.g. specific noun tags NM and NF were mapped to generic noun tag NN). This mapping was restricted to nouns, adjectives and prepositions only as these lexical classes are used to extract term candidates as explained in the following section.

2.3 Term candidate extraction and normalisation

Term candidates are extracted from pre-processed documents using pattern matching. The patterns describe the syntactic structure of targeted noun phrases (NPs). These patterns are treated as parameters of the method and as such can be modified as required. In general, NPs in Welsh and English follow different formation patterns. The main difference is concerned with headedness or directionality of NPs. Nearly all adjectives follow the noun in Welsh (Willis, 2006). For example, *gorsaf ganolog*, where the word *ganolog* means *central*, corresponds to the *central station* in English. Two lexico-syntactic patterns defined using regular expressions were used in our experiments, one to model simple (linear) NPs:

$$NN\ (NN\ |\ JJ)^{+}$$

and the other one to model complex (hierarchical) NPs:

$$NN\ (NN\ |\ JJ)^{*}\ IN\ NN\ (NN\ |\ JJ)^{*}$$

Here, NN, JJ and IN correspond to noun, adjective and preposition respectively.

Identification of term candidates is further refined by trimming the leading and trailing stop words. Stop word list has been created by automatically translating the English stop word list distributed with FlexiTerm (Spasić et al., 2013; Spasić, 2018), e.g. *unrhyw* (Engl. *any*), *bron* (Engl. *nearly*), etc. The translation was performed using the Canolfan Bedwyr Machine Translation Online API (Jones, 2015).

To neutralise morphological and orthographic variation, all term candidates undergo normalisation, which involves lemmatisation of each token and removal of punctuation, numbers, stop words and any lowercase tokens with less than 3 characters. To address syntactic variation, the order is ignored by representing each candidate as a bag of words (BOW). For example, term candidates *niwed i iechyd* (Engl. *damage to health*) and *iechyd niwed* (Engl. *health damage*) are both represented as {*niwed, iechyd*}.

Unlike English, Welsh syntax often requires words to inflect at the beginning depending on the preceding word or its role in the sentence (Harlow, 1989). These morphological changes are known as mutations. For example, *mwg tybaco* (Engl. *tobacco smoke*) can appear as *fwg tybaco* in some contexts where soft mutation occurs. Lemmatisation will neutralise various word mutations. In the previous example, both *mwg* and *fwg* would be lemmatised to *mwg*.

2.4 Lexical similarity

As mentioned before, many types of morphological variation can be neutralised by lemmatisation. For instance, *cerbyd* (Engl. *vehicle*) and *cerbydau* (Engl. *vehicles*) will be conflated to the same lemma *cerbyd*. However, previously normalised term candidates may still contain typographical errors or spelling mistakes. Lexical similarity can be used to conflate these types of variation. For example, two normalised candidates {*llywodraeth, cymru*} and {*llywrydraeth, cymru*} (where *llywrydraeth* is a misspelling of the correct word that means government) can be conflated into the same normalised form {llywodraeth, llywrydraeth, cymru}. In FlexiTerm, similar tokens are matched using the Cysill Ar-Lein (Spelling and Grammar Checker) API (Robertson, 2015).

2.5 Termhood calculation

Calculation of termhood is based on the C-value formula (Frantzi et al., 2000), which is based on the idea of a cost criteria-based measure originally introduced for automatic collocation extraction (Kita et al., 1994):

$$C-value(t) = \begin{cases} \ln |t| \cdot f(t) & , \text{ if } S(t) = \varnothing \\ \ln |t| \cdot (f(t) - \dfrac{1}{|S(t)|} \sum_{s \in S(t)} f(s)) & , \text{ if } S(t) \neq \varnothing \end{cases}$$

In this formula, $|t|$ represents the number of content words in term candidate t, $f(t)$ is the overall frequency of occurrence of term t which aggregates occurrences of the corresponding term variants. $S(t)$ is a set of all other term candidates that are proper

supersets of t. The termhood calculation module is language independent and as such required no modification for Welsh.

2.6 Output

Given a corpus of text documents, FlexiTerm outputs a ranked list of MWTs together with their termhood scores. Within this list, all term variants that share the same normalised form represented as a BOW are grouped together and ordered by their frequency of occurrence. Table 2 provides a sample output. We added English translation manually for the benefit of non-Welsh readers.

Rank	Term variants	Translation	Score
1	mwg ail-law fwg ail-law	second-hand smoking	3.4657
2	fwg tybaco amgylcheddol mwg tybaco amgylcheddol	environmental tobacco smoke	3.2958
3	cerbyd preifat cerbydau preifat	private vehicle	2.7726
4	niwed difrifol i iechyd niwed i iechyd iechyd niwed	damage to health	2.0794
5	Llywodraeth Cymru Lywodraeth Cymru	Welsh Government	1.3863

Table 2: Sample output

3 Results

3.1 Data

We assembled three parallel corpora from three domains: education, politics and health. For each domain, a total of 100 publicly available documents were downloaded from the Welsh Government web site (Welsh Government, 2019). The Welsh Language Act 1993 obliges all public sector bodies to give equal importance to both Welsh and English when delivering services to the public in Wales. This means that all documents we collected from the Welsh Government web site were available in both languages. We collected a total of 100 documents in both languages for each of the three domains considered (600 in total). All documents were pre-processed to remove HTML formatting and stored in a plain text format for further processing by FlexiTerm. Table 3 describes the properties of each corpus whose name consists of two letters – first indicating the language and the second indicating the domain (e.g. WH stands for Welsh+Health).

Data set	Size (KB)	Sentences	Tokens	Distinct lemmas
EE	138	869	24,580	2,517
WE	141	913	27,847	2,204
EP	116	831	21,406	2,444
WP	120	877	23,884	2,352
EH	92	596	16,614	2,063
WH	96	615	18,975	1,960

Table 3: Three parallel domain-specific corpora

3.2 Silver standard

FlexiTerm had previously been thoroughly evaluated for English using the standard measures of precision and recall (Spasić et al., 2013). Their values were calculated against term occurrences that were annotated manually in five corpora used for evaluation. In this particular study, we are focusing on the actual terms extracted as a ranked list and not their specific occurrences in text. This simplifies the evaluation task as it does not require manual annotation of term occurrences in the three corpora (WE, WP and WH). Instead, only the ranked term lists need to be inspected. Moreover, the goal of this study is not to evaluate how well the Welsh version of FlexiTerm performs in general, but rather examine how it compares relative to the English version. In other words, by already knowing the performance of the English version of FlexiTerm from the previous study (Spasić et al., 2013), we can use its output on English versions of the three corpora (EE, EP and EH) as the "silver standard". The results obtained from the Welsh versions of the three corpora (WE, WP and WH) can then be matched against the silver standard. The only manual effort this approach requires is to map each automatically extracted term in Welsh to its equivalent in English (if an equivalent term has been recognised by FlexiTerm) and vice versa. Such mapping was performed by a Welsh-English proficient bilingual speaker.

3.3 Evaluation

We ran two versions of FlexiTerm against the three parallel corpora. Table 4 specifies the number of automatically recognised terms in each language. The Welsh output was evaluated against the corresponding English output (used here as the silver standard) in terms of precision and recall (also specified in Table 4). In other words, to calculate precision, for every Welsh term candidate, we checked whether its equivalent (i.e. translation) appeared in the English output. Vice versa, to calculate recall, for every English term candidate, we checked whether its equivalent appeared in the Welsh output.

	Welsh terms	English terms	P	R	F	κ
Health	90	120	75.0	55.1	63.5	0.6300
Education	107	136	63.8	46.3	53.7	0.8425
Politics	124	127	68.0	65.6	66.8	0.8550
Average	**107**	**128**	**68.9**	**55.7**	**61.3**	**0.7758**

Table 4: Evaluation results

Across the three domains, the Welsh version of FlexiTerm performed more consistently in terms of precision, which was relatively high (i.e. >60%).

However, the recall varied significantly across the three corpora ranging from as low as 46.3% to as high as 65.6%.

3.4 Discussion

We investigated the plausible causes affecting the sensitivity of the method in Welsh, which are associated with different steps of the FlexiTerm algorithm: (1) term candidate selection, (2) term candidate normalisation, (3) termhood calculation.

First, term candidate selection depends on a set of lexico-syntactic patterns. If their coverage does not cover certain term formation patterns, then the corresponding terms will fail to be recognised. For example, the structure NN DT NN of the term *rheoliad y cyngor* (Engl.*council regulation*) does not match any of the patterns specified in Section 2.2, so further investigation is needed into the Welsh term formation patterns.

Furthermore, term candidate selection depends on linguistic pre-processing (see Section 2.1). For example, even if a term's internal structure does comply with the given patterns, for the term to be selected that structure needs to be correctly recognised. In practice, a term's constituents may consistently be tagged incorrectly or ambiguously with POS information. For example, the term *data biometrig* (Engl. *biometric data*) was tagged as NN ? (where ? denotes an unknown tag) instead of NN JJ. Such cases may fail to be matched with any of the given patterns, and, therefore, will also fail to be recognised.

Once term candidates have been selected, their formal recognition as terms will depend on their frequency of occurrence. The overall frequency may be underestimated when different term variants fail to be conflated into a single term representative used to aggregate their individual frequencies. Term conflation depends on term normalisation, which involves (1) lemmatisation of individual words and (2) lexical similarity of their lemmas. The performance of the Welsh lemmatiser was found to be poorer than that of its English counterpart. Further, term normalisation depends on matching lexically similar tokens (see Section 2.4). Welsh orthography uses 29 letters out of which eight are digraphs. Morphology of the words is also more likely to vary than English depending on the dialect (e.g. northern vs. southern dialects). For example, *hogyn* is the northern variant of *bachgen* (Engl. *boy*). While the same approach to term normalisation is still valid for Welsh, it requires further investigation into adjusting the lexical similarity threshold.

Finally, other than frequency, the calculation of the termhood also depends on the length of the term candidate (see Section 2.5). The equivalent terms in the corresponding languages may not necessarily have the same number of content words due to compounding. For example, *ansawdd gofal iechyd* has got three content words whereas its English translation *quality of healthcare* has got two content words. This means that their termhood calculated using the C-value formula may have significantly different values. If this value does not meet the termhood threshold, the candidate will fail to be recognised as a term. In the worst case scenario, a MWT in one language (e.g. *gofal iechyd*) may be a singleton in the other language (e.g. *healthcare*), and as a single-word term it will fail to be identified as a term candidate.

To check how well the respective terminologies are aligned, we compared whether the ranking of terms was similar. The C-value scores are replaced by their rank when they are sorted in the descending order. Note that such ranking represents a weak order because different terms may have the same C-value and, therefore, the same rank. We can view the ranking of terms as an ordinal classification problem. This allows us to compare the differences in the ranking using weighted kappa coefficient (Cohen, 1968), which is traditionally used to calculate inter-annotator agreement. Unlike the original kappa coefficient, the weighted version accounts for the degree of disagreement by assigning different weights w_i to cases where annotations differ by i categories.

We reported the values of this statistics in Table 4 for the terms recognised in both languages. In other words, the missing values, i.e. terms not recognised in one of the languages, were ignored. These values have already been accounted for by means of precision and recall. For the common terms in the domains of education and politics, at $\kappa > 0.8$ the agreement of ranking is almost perfect. In the health domain, the agreement is still substantial at $\kappa > 0.6$.

4 Conclusions

In this paper we presented an adaptation of a MWT recognition algorithm, originally implemented for English, for Welsh. We compared the performance of the Welsh version relative to the original English version. The results demonstrate that the brute-force adaptation, which is concerned only with the modules that support linguistic pre-processing (e.g. POS tagging), will successfully recognise the majority of MWTs proposed by the English version ($P = 68.9\%$, $R = 55.7\%$). It is expected that fine tuning the internal parameters of the method (e.g. lexico-syntactic patterns and lexical similarity threshold) as well as improving the performance of external parameters (e.g. POS tagging) would further improve the performance in Welsh. Successfully

mapping MWTs between Welsh and English would improve the performance of machine translation of specialised texts, whose quality of translation depends largely on using established terminology instead of verbatim translations.

5 Availability

The software is shared under the BSD-3-clause license on GitHub:

https://github.com/ispasic/FlexiTermCymraeg

References

Arppe, A. (1995) Term Extraction from Unrestricted Text. 10th Nordic Conference of Computational Linguistics, Helsinki, Finland

Cohen, J. (1968) Weighted kappa: nominal scale agreement with provision for scaled disagreement or partial credit. Psychol Bull 70(4):213-20.

Daille, B. (1996). Study and implementation of combined techniques for automatic extraction of terminology. In P. Resnik & J. Klavans (Eds.), The Balancing Act - Combining Symbolic and Statistical Approaches to Language, MIT Press, 49-66.

Frantzi K., Ananiadou S. (1997) Automatic term recognition using contextual cues. 3rd DELOS Workshop on Cross-Language Information Retrieval, Zurich, Switzerland.

Frantzi, K., Ananiadou, S., Mima, H. (2000). Automatic recognition of multi-word terms: the C-value/NC-value method. International Journal on Digital Libraries 2000, 3:115–130.

Harlow, S. (1989) The syntax of Welsh soft mutation. Natural Language & Linguistic Theory 7(3):289–316.

Hersh, W., Campbell, E., Malveau, S., (1997). Assessing the feasibility of largescale natural language processing in a corpus of ordinary medical records: a lexical analysis. Annual AMIA Fall Symposium, 580–584.

Jacquemin, C. (2001). Spotting and Discovering Terms through Natural Language Processing. Cambridge, Massachusetts, USA: MIT Press.

Jones, D.B. (2015). Machine Translation Online API [https://github.com/PorthTechnolegauIaith/moses-smt/blob/master/docs/APIArlein.md#moses-smt-machine-translation-online-api].

Jones, D. B., Robertson, P., Prys, G. (2015) Welsh language lemmatizer API service [http://techiaith.cymru/api/lemmatizer/?lang=en].

Jones, D. B., Robertson, P., Prys, G. (2015). Welsh language Parts-of-Speech Tagger API Service [http://techiaith.cymru/api/parts-of-speech-tagger-api/?lang=en].

Justeson, J. S., Katz, S. M. (1995) Technical terminology: some linguistic properties and an algorithm for identification in text. Natural Language Engineering 1(1): 9-27.

Kageura, K., Umino, B. (1996). Methods of automatic term recognition - A review. Terminology 3(2): 259-289.

Kita K, Y. Kato, T. Omoto and Y. Yano (1994) A comparative study of automatic extraction of collocations from corpora: Mutual information vs. cost criteria. Journal of Natural Language Processing 1:21-33.

Nattinger, J., DeCarrico, J. (2011) Lexical phrases and language teaching. Oxford University Press.

Robertson, P. (2015). Cysill Ar-lein [https://github.com/PorthTechnolegauIaith/cysill/blob/master/doc/README.md#cysill-online-api].

Robertson, P. (2015). POS Tagger API [https://github.com/PorthTechnolegauIaith/postagger/blob/master/doc/README.md#results].

Smadja, F. (1993) Retrieving collocations from text: Xtract. Computational Linguistics 19(1):143-177.

Spasić, I., Greenwood, M., Preece, A., Francis, N., Elwyn, G. (2013) FlexiTerm: a flexible term recognition method. Journal of Biomedical Semantics 4: 27.

Spasić, I. (2018) Acronyms as an integral part of multi-word term recognition - A token of appreciation. IEEE Access 6: 8351-8363.

Spasić, I., Corcoran, P., Gagarin, A., Buerki, A. (2018) Head to head: Semantic similarity of multi-word terms. IEEE Access 6: 20545-20557.

Toutanova, K., Klein, D., Manning, C., Singer, Y. (2003) Feature-rich part-of-speech tagging with a cyclic dependency network. North American Chapter of the Association for Computational Linguistics on Human Language Technology, 173-180.

Welsh Government (2019). Catalog Cyhoeddiadau Llywodraeth Cymru / Welsh Government Publications Catalogue

[http://welshgovernmentpublications.soutron.net/publications/]

Willis, D. (2006) Against N-raising and NP-raising analyses of Welsh noun phrases. Lingua 116(11): 1807-1839.

Universal dependencies for Scottish Gaelic: syntax

Colin Batchelor

Royal Society of Chemistry, Thomas Graham House, Cambridge, UK CB4 0WF

`colin.r.batchelor@gmail.com`

Abstract

We present universal dependencies for Scottish Gaelic and a treebank of 1021 sentences (20 021 tokens) drawn from the Annotated Reference Corpus Of Scottish Gaelic (ARCOSG). The tokens are annotated for coarse part-of-speech, fine-grained part-of-speech, syntactic features and dependency relations. We discuss how the annotations differ from the treebanks developed for two other Celtic languages, Irish and Breton, and in preliminary dependency parsing experiments we obtain a mean labelled attachment score of 0.792. We also discuss some difficult cases for future investigation, including cosubordination. The treebank is available, along with documentation, from `https://universaldependencies.org/`.

1 Introduction

Scottish Gaelic is an low-resourced language which has hitherto lacked a robust parser, despite the recent development of the Annotated Reference Corpus of Scottish Gaelic (ARCOSG) (Lamb et al., 2016). Previous work (Batchelor, 2016) has leveraged ARCOSG to produce a medium-coverage categorial grammar but not a gold standard corpus that would enable the grammar to be properly evaluated. In this work we fill this gap by creating a dependency treebank for Scottish Gaelic of similar size to the existing treebanks in Irish (Lynn, 2016) and (Lynn and Foster, 2016) and Breton (Tyers and Ravishankar, 2018). An

© 2019 The authors. This article is licensed under a Creative Commons 4.0 licence, no derivative works, attribution, CC-BY-ND.

important advantage of the dependency grammar approach is that the tools are better developed and less closely tied to English than for combinatory categorial grammar (CCG). Indeed, the universal dependencies (UD) framework has been developed to cover as wide a range of languages as possible, and recent CoNLL shared tasks have been explicitly multilingual, for example the 2018 task which focussed on extracting universal dependencies for 82 treebanks in 57 languages (Zeman et al., 2018). Given a corpus in CoNLL format, the udpipe package (Straka and Straková, 2017) can be used to train a tokeniser, a POS tagger and a dependency parser. In this work we will concentrate on the last of these and present preliminary results.

2 Scottish Gaelic

Scottish Gaelic, hereafter Gaelic, is a Celtic language of the Goidelic family closely related to Irish and Manx. It is spoken mainly in the Highlands and islands of Scotland, in the cities of the Central Belt and in Cape Breton in Canada. Its usage has been declining since the Middle Ages, when placename evidence attests its presence as far southeast as Fife and even East Lothian (Gullane, Innerwick and Ballencrieff all have Gaelic etymologies) and according to the UNESCO Atlas of the World's Languages in Danger it is "definitely endangered" (Moseley, 2010). Lamb (2003) has published an accessible grammar of the language, but for a fuller account see Cox (2017) and for a short practical account focussing on contemporary usage see Ross et al. (2019).

The main electronic corpora for the language are ARCOSG and *Corpas na Gàidhlig* 'Corpus of Gaelic', part of the Digital Archive of Scottish Gaelic (DASG) (University of Glasgow, 2019).

The usual word order is VSO, but periphrastic

constructions are very common and in contrast to Irish the usual way of expressing that something is taking place in the present is to use the verb *bi* and the verbal noun, for example *Tha mi a' dol* 'I am at going' for 'I am going'. We will discuss other differences from Irish, mainly that certain constructions are much more common in one language than the other, in more depth later on. There are two genders (masculine and feminine), three numbers (singular, plural and a separate dual form for nouns) and four cases (nominative, vocative, genitive and dative). Like the other Celtic languages Gaelic has conjugated prepositions such as *agam* 'at me' and *oirnn* 'on us'. These were already single words by the time of Old Irish (the 8th and 9th centuries CE) (Stifter, 2006). Both Irish and Scottish Gaelic exhibit cosubordination (Lamb, 2003). This is where the coordinator *agus* is followed by a nominal subject and an adjectival predicate or a small clause. Usually in Scottish Gaelic the cosubordinated clause follows the main clause, but it is not unusual in Irish to see it fronted. We will discuss options for handling this later on. Lastly, it is very common to express psychological states by a combination of the verb *bi*, a noun and two prepositional phrases, for example 'I love her' is *Tha gaol agam oirre* 'There is love at me on her'.

3 Related work

The first work on a dependency treebank for Gaelic was by Batchelor (2014) which predated the release of ARCOSG and was built from a tiny collection (82 sentences) of hand-picked sentences. At the same time Lamb and Danso presented a part-of-speech tagger for Gaelic based on ARCOSG (Lamb and Danso, 2014). Subsequently Tyers and Ravishankar (2018) have presented a Universal Dependencies treebank for Breton.

4 Corpus

ARCOSG is a corpus of 76 texts from a variety of genres, including conversations, sports commentary, fiction and news. Part of the context for the development of ARCOSG is given in (Lamb, 1999) where Lamb describes the development of the news reports and the language used on Radio nan Gàidheal. The texts have been part-of-speech tagged by hand according to a tagging scheme described in (2014) and based on the PAROLE tagset used by Uí Dhonnchadha (2009).

ARCOSG is made available in Brown Corpus format. This is converted into CoNLL-U format with a short Python script and the fine-grained part-of-speech tags mapped to the coarse-grained UD v2 tagset. A sample of the mapping is shown in Table 1. The LEMMA field in the treebank is populated using an extended version of the lemmatiser described in Batchelor (2016). The FEATS field is populated in the conversion process, largely following the feature set for Irish (Lynn et al., 2017). The corpus is broken into sentences on full stops and sentence boundaries corrected in manual postprocessing.

We use the texts in the following subcorpora: narrative, news, fiction, formal prose and popular writing. We have initially excluded the conversation and interview subcorpora because of the large fraction of single-token utterances. We also exclude the sports subcorpus for the moment as it largely consists of highly paratactic football commentary. Table 2 gives an overview. 752 sentences (25 593 tokens) remain to be added to the corpus and 30 sentences (1043 tokens) are awaiting a better treatment of cosubordination. Lastly there are five sentences in the narrative subcorpus which have a total of 5092 tokens between them.

5 Annotation

In this section we describe the process and look at some special cases in the light of the Irish and Breton treebanks.

5.1 Guidelines

We use the generic Universal Dependencies guidelines (Universal Dependencies contributors, 2016) and refer to the Irish UD corpus (Lynn and Foster, 2016) and our own list of special cases[1] in case of doubt. There is a single human annotator, an experienced adult learner of Gaelic, but the tagset used in ARCOSG is extremely rich, with well over 200 POS tags and marks for tense, case, number and gender and hence does a great deal of disambiguation. We follow Lynn et al. (2013) in marking up a small portion of the corpus (around 1000 tokens in this case) by hand and then iteratively training MaltParser (Nivre et al., 2006) with the standard settings on an annotated/checked part of the corpus and using it to parse the unchecked part. We

---

[1]See `guidelines.md` and the documentation for the python conversion scripts in `https://github.com/colinbatchelor/gdbank/releases/tag/v0.2-alpha`

ARCOSG	UD	Comments	Examples
A*	ADJ	adjectives	
Dd	DET	determiners	*seo* 'this', *ud* 'yon'
Dp*	DET	possessive pronouns	*mo* 'my'
Dq	DET	determiners	*gach* 'every', *a h-uile* 'every'
Cc	CCONJ	coordinators	*agus* 'and', *ach* 'but', *oir* 'for'
Cs	SCONJ	subordinators	*ged* 'although', *nuair* 'when'
F*	PUNCT	punctuation	
I	INTJ	interjections	*O* 'oh', *Seadh* 'aye', *Uill* 'well'
M*	NUM	numbers (non-human series)	
Nc*	NOUN	common nouns	
Nf	ADP	fossilized nouns	*airson* 'for', *air feadh* 'throughout'
Nn*	PROPN	proper nouns	
Nt	PROPN	toponyms	
Nv	NOUN	verbal nouns	*lorg* 'going'
Pp*	PRON	personal pronouns	*mi* 'I'
Pr*	ADP	conjugated prepositions	*orm* 'on me', *aige-san* 'at him'
Q*	PART	particles	*a* (relativiser), *cha* (negative particle)
R*	ADV	adverbs	*a-mach* 'out', *cuideachd* 'also'
Sa	PART	aspectual markers	*a'*, *ag*, *ri*
Sp	ADP	prepositions	*aig* 'at'
Td*	DET	articles	*an*, *na*, *nan* 'the', 'of the'
U*	PART	particles	*a* (adverbialiser), *a* (vocative)
Uf	NOUN	fossilized nouns	*'S urrainn* 'can', *'S dòcha* 'maybe'
Um	ADP	'than'	*na*
Uo	PART	numerical prefix	*a naoi* 'nine' (but see below for *h-*, *n-*, *t-*)
Up	PROPN	part of proper name	*Mac*
Uq	—	interrogatives	*Dè* 'what' (PRON), *Ciamar* 'how' (ADV)
V*	VERB	verb	
W*	AUX	copula	*B'* 'was', *'sann* (see below)
Xfe	—	foreign word	X for running text, NOUN where foreign noun
Y	NOUN	abbreviation	*Mgr* 'Mr', *a BhBC* 'of the BBC'

Table 1: Mapping of the most important part-of-speech classes from ARCOSG to the UD coarse-grained tagset. The asterisk in A*, for example, indicates that all of the tags beginning with A map on to ADJ.

proofread the trees, add them to the training data, and iteratively improve the unchecked portion of the corpus. We keep trees which feature cosubordination in a separate file for future work.

5.2 Tokenisation

By and large we follow the tokenisation in AR-COSG but we do have to make some adjustments to match the UD scheme. Firstly, ARCOSG treats a number of multiword expressions such as place-names and the prepositions *ann an*, *anns an*, 'in', 'in the' and variants as a single token. We retokenise these on whitespace and assign, for the moment, the same part-of-speech tag to all of them. Secondly the prefixes *h-*, *n-* and *t-*, which are in-

separable parts of the word written without a hyphen in Irish, are treated as independent tokens with type Uo. These we unite with the tokens that follow them into a single token. There is a small number of multitoken compound prepositions that according to ARCOSG are three tokens, including a punctuation mark, for example *a-rèir* 'according to', which we collapse into a single token.

In addition we have to make some assumptions about reconstructing the original text, which is absent from the corpus. To this end we use the Gaelic Orthographic Conventions (GOC) ((SQA), 2009) for consistency in reconstructing spacing, but don't apply any other corrections. We retain spaces after *a'*, *b'*, *d'*, *m'*, *th'* and *bh'*. If an elided *a'* or

Subcorpus	# sentences	Mean # tokens	Longest	Shortest
Fiction	397	17.0	61	2
Formal prose	120	24.9	113	5
News	167	22.2	52	7
Narrative	132	18.2	112	3
Popular writing	205	20.4	59	4

Table 2: Overview of the subset of ARCOSG in the treebank.

ag before a verbal noun is indicated by ', this is combined with the following token.

We make limited use of UD's word–token distinction at present. The Irish and Breton treebanks differ on how to treat conjugated prepositions, with Breton dividing the single token *ganto* 'with them' into two words, *gant* and *o*, and Irish keeping *orm* 'on me' as a single word rather than dividing it into *ar* and *mé*. We follow the Irish example, but do divide tokens that have been tagged as fused tokens by ARCOSG. One example of this is *cuimhneam* 'memory at me', which has the POS `Ncsfn+Pr1s` (singular feminine common noun and first person singular conjugated preposition). In this case we divide it into the two words *cuimhne* and *agam*. There are currently ten examples of this in the treebank.

5.3 Personal names

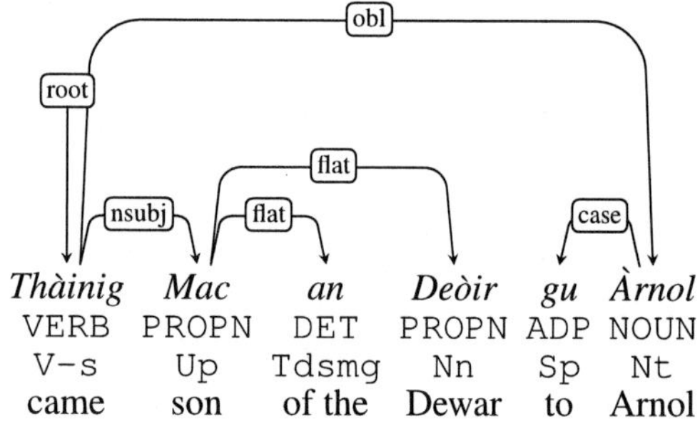

Figure 1: 'Dewar came to Arnol' (part of tree pw05_017), showing how compound proper names are handled.

We treat personal names, following the UD v2 guidelines, as a flat structure even in the case of surnames such as *Mac an Deòir* 'Dewar' that have internal grammatical structure (Fig. 1).

5.4 Copular constructions

An important use of the `fixed` relation is for the 'dummy' pronouns *e* and *ann* in the copular constructions *'s e*, *b' e*, *'s ann* and *b' ann*, which are sometimes written as a single word. Two examples

are given in Fig. 2. *'S e* (or in this case *'S i*) introduces an NP, and *'S ann* (or *'Sann*) is used for other sorts of constituent, here *an Ìle*, 'in Islay'. The expression that follows the dummy pronoun as being the root of the clause, and the expression that follows that as the subject. It may be a definite NP, in which case we use the relation `nsubj`, or clausal, where we use `csubj:cop`. This is broadly similar to the Irish treebank except that Irish does not usually have the dummy pronouns.

5.5 The verbal noun and inversion structures

The verbal noun is intermediate between an archetypal verb and an archetypal noun. In some ways it behaves like a noun. It can be qualified by an adjective preceding it, and in progressive tenses, the NPs governed by a verbal noun were historically always in the genitive, however Ross et al. (2019) say that the genitive 'is no longer required' for indefinite singular nouns in these cases. Equally, it is part of a clause. In the Irish treebank verbal nouns are tagged as `NOUN` and treated as `xcomp` (externally-controlled clausal complements) of the controlling verb. Conversely in the Breton treebank they are tagged as `VERB` and treated as the root, with what would be the controlling verb in Irish treated as `aux` (an auxiliary). The approach where the verbal noun is tagged as a `NOUN` and the controlling verb as `AUX` is disallowed by the validation script. We have chosen to follow the Irish scheme, though these contrasting approaches, shown in Figure 3, both have their merits.

The two main ways of indicating the passive in Scottish Gaelic are synthetic: *Rugadh is thogadh mi* 'I was born and raised' (Fig. 4) and analytic: *Chaidh a' nighean a lorg mu ochd uairean a-raoir.* 'The girl was found about eight o'clock last night'. In the latter case we treat the subject *nighean* as a dependent of the verbal noun *lorg*. The root of the clause is the verb *Chaidh* 'went'. This is shown in Fig. 5. This is different from the approach in

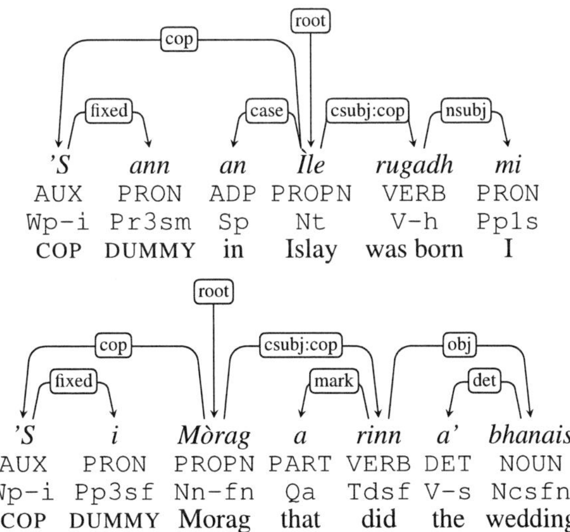

Figure 2: Dependency trees for 'It was in Islay that I was born' and 'It was Morag who had the wedding'.

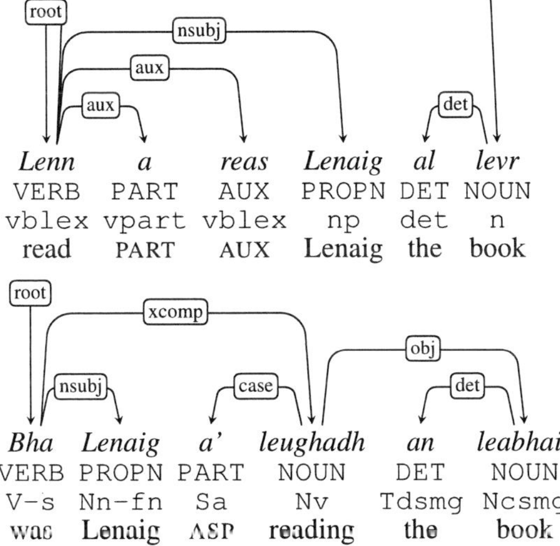

Figure 3: Dependency trees for 'Lenaig read the book' in the Breton (sentence ID grammar.vislcg.txt:28:654) and 'Lenaig was reading the book' in the Gaelic approach.

English where the word 'was' is treated as an auxiliary and the verb 'found' treated as the root, and of course from the Breton example above, but is identical to the other 'inversion' structures in Scottish Gaelic, where the object goes before the verbal noun (Ross et al., 2019), for example obligation: *Feumaidh mi cofaidh òl* 'I must drink coffee', or possibility: *Is urrainn dhuinn an duine a chuideachadh* 'We can help the person'.

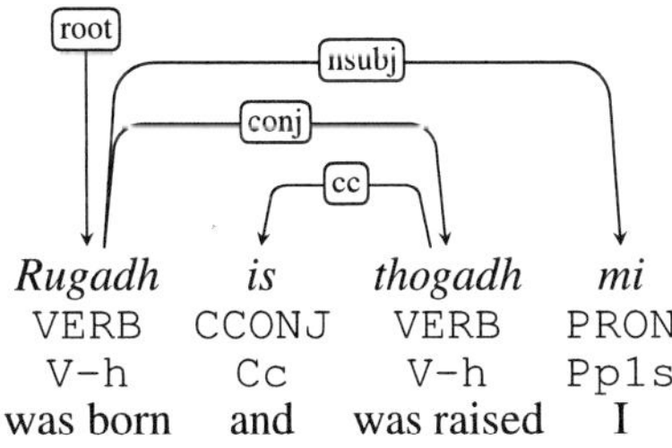

Figure 4: Dependency tree for 'I was born and raised' (analytic passive).

5.6 Numbers

As in Irish, there are two sets of cardinal numbers, one for people and the other for everything else. In ARCOSG *triùir* 'three people' is tagged as a noun (Ncsfn), and *triùir mhac* 'three sons' as Ncsfn Ncpmg. For this reason we treat *triùir* as the content word and *mhac* as a modifier. This is one of the many non-possessive constructions in Gaelic where a noun in the genitive modifies another noun, so we do not follow Breton in using the nmod:poss relation in these cases. Cardinal numbers on the other hand are tagged as Mc and we treat them as modifying their nominal head (nummod) unless they are the subject, object or oblique argument. See Figure 7 for examples.

5.7 Cosubordination

Cosubordination is an important grammatical phenomenon in Gaelic, found in all registers, and it is not clear how to cover it from the UD guidelines. Here is an example, a simplified version of sen-

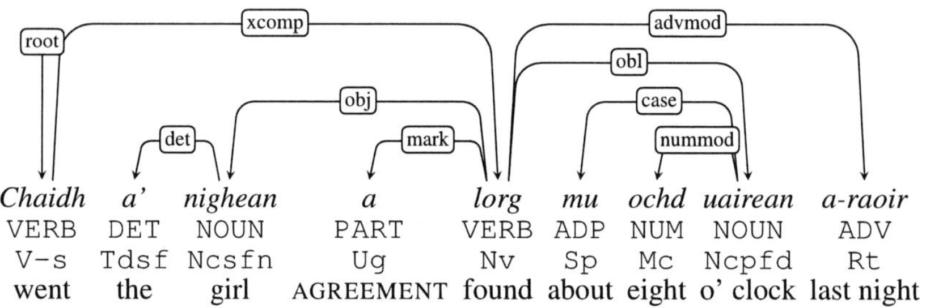

Figure 5: Dependency tree for 'The girl was found about eight o' clock last night' (analytic passive, simplified version of ns10_021 in the as-yet unchecked part of the corpus).

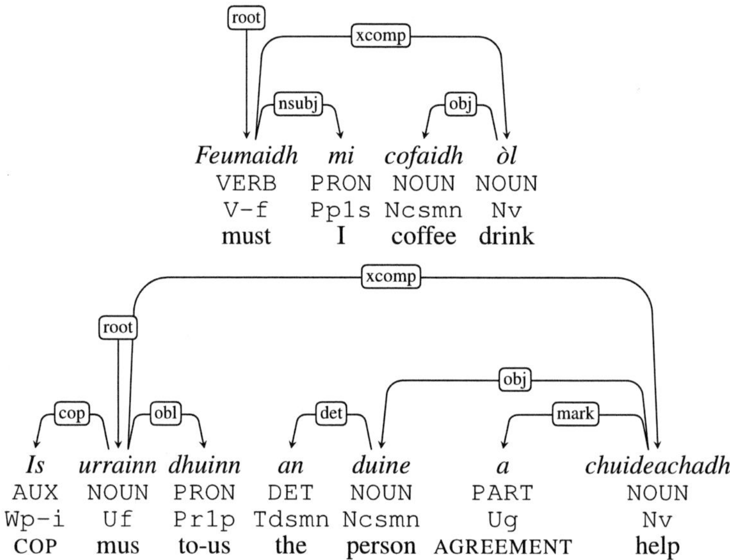

Figure 6: Dependency trees for inversion structures (Ross et al., 2019): 'I must drink coffee' and 'We can help the person'.

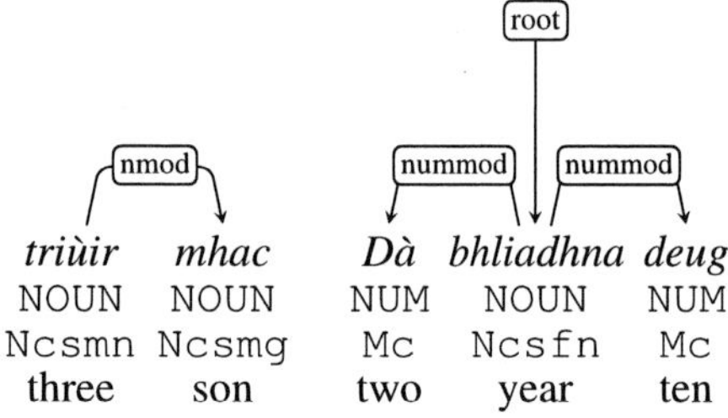

Figure 7: Contrasting treatments of personal numbers (left, from n05_009) and impersonal numbers (right, f08_036).

tence n05_004: *Chaidh e air chall ann an ceò, 's e 'g iasgach.* 'He went missing in the fog when he was fishing', or more literally 'He went missing in the fog, and he fishing'.

We illustrate two approaches in Figure 8. The first one is to use the adnominal clause modifier (`acl`) relation as in the depictive example in the UD guidelines 'She entered the room sad'. This

introduces a non-projective arc between the words *e* 'he' in each clause. The analogous sentence in English is projective because of SVO word order instead of VSO. It would perhaps be clearer to sub-class the pertinent relations as `conj:cosub` and `acl:cosub`. The second approach is to assume that the word *bha* has been elided. This has two advantages: firstly clear UD guidelines, indicating that the correct thing to do is to treat *e* as a conjugate of the root verb *Chaidh* 'went' and connect it to the verbal noun with the `orphan` relation, and secondly maintaining a projective structure. And yet it is not obvious that cosubordination actually is ellipsis. One argument that it isn't is that while in Gaelic the cosubordinate clause usually appears after the main clause, it is not uncommon in Irish to see preposed cosubordinate clauses, for example the phrase *Agus mé óg* 'When I was young'.

The chief drawback of the depictive approach as opposed to the elliptical is non-projectivity, but we

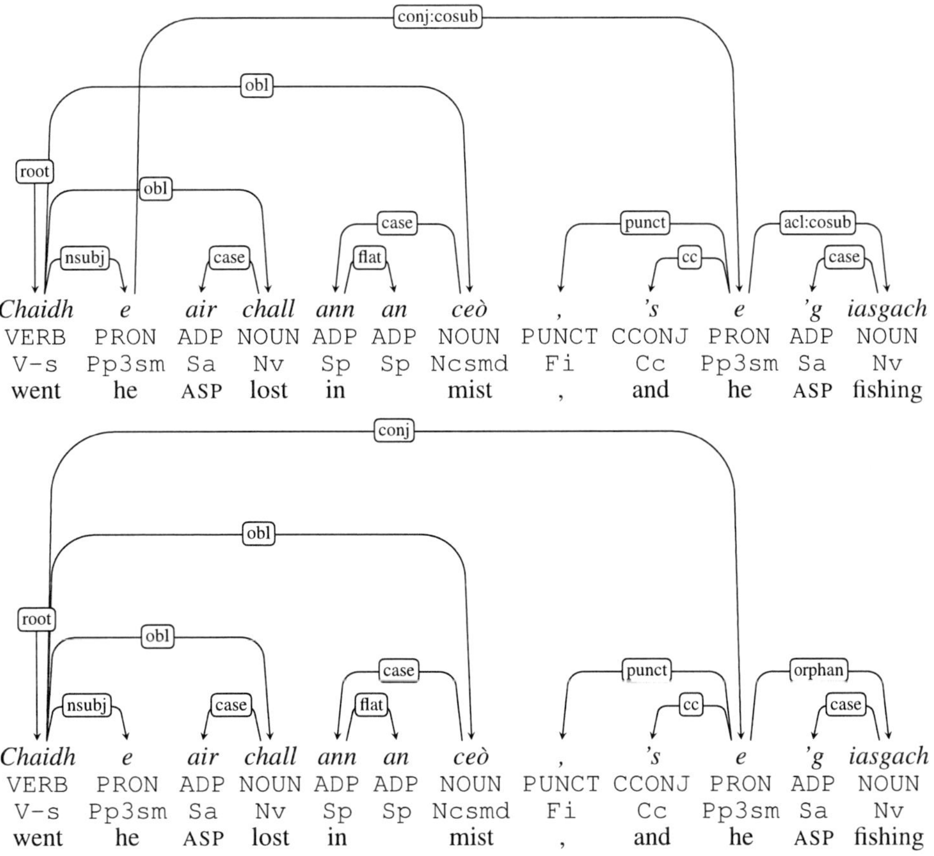

Figure 8: Two approaches to cosubordination. (above) Depictive (below) elliptical.

feel that it is better in terms both of representing the language as it is found in all registers, and in the specificity of the relation used: `acl` as opposed to the more generic `orphan`. A full investigation of how common non-projectivity is in the treebank as a whole should help decide how much weight to place on projectivity as a criterion for annotation choices.

6 Experiments

Transition system	LAS
`projective`	**0.796** [0.752, 0.839]
`swap` (non-projective)	0.789 [0.747, 0.825]
`link2` (non-projective)	0.792 [0.750, 0.835]

Table 3: Labelled-attachment scores (LAS) for parsing the treebank with different transition systems for udpipe's parsito parser. The LAS are the mean values from ten-fold cross-validation. There were 1021 sentences and 20 031 words.

In this section we examine briefly how learnable the annotation scheme is by a dependency parser and the effects of different parsing algorithms. A fuller account awaits a larger treebank, which on average will have longer sentences. Because of the small size of the corpus we use ten-fold cross validation. We use udpipe's parsito parser and MaltEval (Nilsson and Nivre, 2008), both with the default settings. Table 3 gives the ten-fold cross-validated labelled-attachment scores (LAS) for the three transition systems, one projective and two non-projective. We find that the default, projective transition system performs best, with a mean LAS of 0.796, but the three are very similar, and the scores may be flattered by the relatively short mean sentence length (19.6 words). These scores are comparable to the scores for much larger treebanks given by Nivre and Fang (2017).

7 Conclusions and future work

This is the first reasonably-sized dependency treebank of Scottish Gaelic and the first demonstration of a fast parser for the language. The treebank can also be used for tokenisation and part-of-speech tagging using udpipe, though as mentioned before the tokenisation scheme is different from that used in ARCOSG.

The treebank presented here is not quite ready for an official release, despite its passing the validation script. Nonetheless a significant part of the treebanking process, annotating a part-of-speech corpus with lemmas, universal part-of-speech tags, syntactic features and dependency relations, has been achieved. A substantial part of ARCOSG has not been covered in this work—the conversation, sport and interview subcorpora, and five of the texts in the narrative subcorpus. There are also over 750 trees that are not yet in the treebank but they will be processed in due course. Lastly, given the close relation between the two languages and that the annotation scheme presented here is as close as possible to the Irish one, it would be very interesting to repeat the parsing experiments on a combined Irish and Scottish Gaelic corpus.

References

Batchelor, Colin. 2014. gdbank: The beginnings of a corpus of dependency structures and type-logical grammar in Scottish Gaelic. In *Proceedings of the First Celtic Language Technology Workshop*, pages 60–65, Dublin, Ireland, August. Association for Computational Linguistics and Dublin City University.

Batchelor, Colin. 2016. Automatic derivation of categorial grammar from a part-of-speech-tagged corpus in Scottish Gaelic. In *Actes de la conférence conjointe JEP-TALN-RECITAL 2016, volume 6 : CLTW*, Paris, France, July.

Cox, Richard A. V. 2017. *Geàrr-Ghràmar na Gàidhlig*. Clann Tuirc, Tigh a' Mhaide, Ceann Drochaid, Alba.

Lamb, William and Samuel Danso. 2014. Developing an Automatic Part-of-Speech Tagger for Scottish Gaelic. In *Proceedings of the First Celtic Language Technology Workshop*, pages 1–5, Dublin, Ireland, August. Association for Computational Linguistics and Dublin City University.

Lamb, William, Sharon Arbuthnot, Susanna Naismith, and Samuel Danso. 2016. Annotated Reference Corpus of Scottish Gaelic (ARCOSG), 1997–2016 [dataset]. Technical report, University of Edinburgh; School of Literatures, Languages and Cultures; Celtic and Scottish Studies. http://dx. doi.org/10.7488/ds/1411.

Lamb, William. 1999. A diachronic account of Gaelic news-speak: The development and expansion of a register. *Scottish Gaelic Studies*, XIX:141–171.

Lamb, William. 2003. *Scottish Gaelic, 2nd edn*. Lincom Europa, Munich, Germany.

Lynn, Teresa and Jennifer Foster. 2016. Universal Dependencies for Irish. In *Actes de la conférence conjointe JEP-TALN-RECITAL 2016, volume 6 : CLTW*, Paris, France, July.

Lynn, Teresa, Jennifer Foster, and Mark Dras. 2013. Working with a small dataset - semi-supervised dependency parsing for Irish. In *Proceedings of the Fourth Workshop on Statistical Parsing of Morphologically-Rich Languages*, pages 1–11, Seattle, Washington, USA, October. Association for Computational Linguistics.

Lynn, Teresa, Jennifer Foster, and Mark Dras. 2017. Morphological Features of the Irish Universal Dependency Treebank. In *TLT 2017: Proceedings of the 15th International Workshop on Treebanks and Linguistic Theories*, Aachen, Germany.

Lynn, Teresa. 2016. *Irish Dependency Treebanking and Parsing*. Ph.D. thesis, Dublin City University and Macquarie University.

Moseley, Christopher, editor. 2010. *Atlas of the World's Languages in Danger*. UNESCO Publishing, Paris, 3rd edition.

Naismith, Susanna and William Lamb. 2014. Scottish Gaelic Part-of-Speech Annotation Guidelines. Celtic and Scottish Studies, University of Edinburgh.

Nilsson, Jens and Joakim Nivre. 2008. MaltEval: an evaluation and visualization tool for dependency parsing. In *LREC 2008*.

Nivre, Joakim and Chiao-Ting Fang. 2017. Universal dependency evaluation. In *Proceedings of the NoDaLiDa 2017 Workshop on Universal Dependencies (UDW 2017)*, pages 86–95, Gothenburg, Sweden, May. Association for Computational Linguistics.

Nivre, Joakim, Johan Hall, and Jens Nilsson. 2006. MaltParser: A data-driven parser-generator for dependency parsing. In *Proceedings of the Fifth International Conference on Language Resources and Evaluation (LREC'06)*, Genoa, Italy, May. European Language Resources Association (ELRA).

Ross, Susan, Mark McConville, Wilson McLeod, and Richard Cox. 2019. Stiùireadh Gràmair. https://dasg.ac.uk/grammar/grammar.pdf, accessed 23 May 2019.

(SQA), Scottish Qualifications Authority. 2009. *Gaelic Orthographic Conventions*. Scottish Qualifications Authority, Dalkeith.

Stifter, David. 2006. *Sengoidelc: Old Irish for beginners*. Syracuse University Press, Syracuse, New York.

Straka, Milan and Jana Straková. 2017. Tokenizing, pos tagging, lemmatizing and parsing ud 2.0 with udpipe. In *Proceedings of the CoNLL 2017 Shared Task: Multilingual Parsing from Raw Text to Universal Dependencies*, pages 88–99, Vancouver, Canada, August. Association for Computational Linguistics.

Tyers, Francis M. and Vinit Ravishankar. 2018. A prototype dependency treebank for Breton. In *Actes de la conférence Traitement Automatique de la Langue-Naturelle, TALN 2018 : Volume 1 : Articles longs, articles courts de TALN*, pages 197–204, Rennes, France, May.

Uí Dhonnchadha, Elaine. 2009. *Part-of-speech tagging and partial parsing for Irish using finite-state transducers and constraint grammar*. Ph.D. thesis, Dublin City University.

Universal Dependencies contributors. 2016. UD Guidelines, `https://universaldependencies.org/guidelines.html`. Accessed 9 July 2019.

University of Glasgow. 2019. Corpas na Gàidhlig, Digital Archive of Scottish Gaelic (DASG), `https://dasg.ac.uk/corpus/`. Accessed 9 July 2019.

Zeman, Daniel, Jan Hajič, Martin Popel, Martin Potthast, Milan Straka, Filip Ginter, Joakim Nivre, and Slav Petrov. 2018. CoNLL 2018 shared task: Multilingual parsing from raw text to universal dependencies. In *Proceedings of the CoNLL 2018 Shared Task: Multilingual Parsing from Raw Text to Universal Dependencies*, pages 1–21, Brussels, Belgium, October. Association for Computational Linguistics.

Speech technology and Argentinean Welsh

Elise Bell
The University of Texas at El Paso
eabell2@utep.edu

Abstract

This paper argues for increased efforts to source Welsh language data from the population of Welsh speakers in Argentina. The dialect of Argentinean Welsh is under-resourced even in comparison to other Celtic languages, which are already considered less-resourced languages (LRLs). Argentinean Welsh has been shown to diverge from other dialects of Welsh in the realization of acoustic contrasts such as voice-onset time and vowel duration. These differences potentially obscure phonemic contrasts in the language, creating homophony absent in other dialects. The inclusion of Argentinean Welsh data in training sets for future Welsh speech technology development will increase the applicability of such technology to other speaker communities whose Welsh speech may not align with that currently in use for model training, including second-language and non-fluent speakers.

1 Introduction

The development of speech language technology such as automatic speech recognition (ASR) depends on the availability and accessibility of large-scale language data sets, both spoken and written. The information in these data sets is used to create statistical generalizations that form the basis for speech technologies including speech recognition, text-to-speech systems, and grammatical parsing. Large resources of this type are less available for under-resourced languages, including Welsh and other Celtic languages, making creation of speech technologies for these languages more challenging. As we undertake that challenge, it is vital that we consider the source of the data on which our technology is based. As less-resourced language speech technology becomes more broadly accessible, speakers who deviate from the norms explicitly or implicitly assumed by the technology will begin to come in contact with it. Depending on the variety inherent in the data underlying the system, those marginalized speakers may or may not be able to successfully take advantage of speech technology. The aim of this paper is to highlight the particular areas of speech technology development that may create obstacles or pose problems for users, and to propose the addition of a particular source of acoustic data that lies outside the norm for Welsh language technology. The main speaker group of concern here is speakers of Welsh in Argentina, but the arguments that follow apply to second language (L2) or non-fluent speakers of Welsh as well.

Compared to dialects of Welsh spoken in Wales, Argentinean (or Patagonian) Welsh is extremely under-resourced and under-researched. Documentation efforts amount to a handful of citations (Jones, 1984; Jones, 1998; Sleeper, 2015; Bell, 2017), and to my knowledge, only one speech corpus. Little is known about how the dialect of Welsh spoken in Argentina differs from other dialects of Welsh, although there are several reasons to expect dialectal variation. The effects of bilingualism on speech production are well documented (Flege et al., 1997; Flege et al., 2003; Escudero, 2009), and all adult speakers of Argentinean Welsh are bilingual with Spanish (if not trilingual with English or another language). Dialect differences may also

© 2019 The authors. This article is licensed under a Creative Commons 4.0 licence, no derivative works, attribution, CC-BY-ND.

arise from the effects of second language (L2) acquisition of Welsh. Differences in speech production due to these effects may include the merging of phonemic categories, or the use of different acoustic cues in contrast production. Because these effects are fairly inextricably tied up with the effect of Spanish bilingualism on Argentinean Welsh in general, they will not be treated separately here. This paper presents a brief overview of the state of Welsh language speech technology and resources, followed by a short discussion of the history and modern context of the Welsh language in Argentina. Subsequently, I present evidence that experimentally observed differences between Welsh dialects support the inclusion of Argentinean Welsh data in future speech technology development efforts.

1.1 Welsh speech technology

Speech recognition and speech synthesis technologies rely on (relatively) large amounts of acoustic data, which must be transcribed orthographically (in the case of a grapheme-based speech recognition system) or phonetically (in the case of a phoneme-based system). The collection, analysis, and processing of this data requires resources including people-hours, funding, and often, participation of community members in data crowd-sourcing efforts (Prys and Jones, 2018). Currently, available Welsh speech technology is fairly limited (compared to larger-resourced languages like English). Much of what is available has been produced by the Welsh Language Technologies Unit, based at Bangor University.[1] Tools produced by the Language Technologies Unit range from front-end resources accessible to the public (a vocabulary website plugin (Jones et al., 2016), a Welsh language spelling and grammar checker (Prys et al., 2016)) to back-end tools such as a part-of-speech tagger (Prys and Jones, 2015) that are open source and accessible to researchers outside of the unit itself. The unit has also developed speech recognition and synthetic speech technologies that are of particular relevance to this paper. These include the development of Macsen,[2] a Welsh-language personal digital assistant based on data collected by the Languages Technologies Unit

using the Paldaruo app[3] and website to crowd-source the collection of Welsh utterances (Prys and Jones, 2018). Utterances were elicited with a set of target words and sentences designed to collect a representative phoneme set. The project is currently available through the Mozilla Common-Voice project[4] where users can contribute and evaluate recordings, and where a portion of the vetted data is available for download.

There are several other text and speech corpora available for the Welsh language. The Language Technologies Unit has created multiple text corpora, including one of social media posts[5] as well as a million-word corpus consisting of various registers of Welsh writing.[6] Researchers at Bangor University's ESRC Centre for Research on Bilingualism in Theory & Practice have also produced two publicly available corpora of Welsh bilingual speech.[7] One of these, the Patagonia corpus, is to my knowledge the only publicly available collection of Argentinean Welsh speech. While such conversational corpora are invaluable for the study of syntactic and morphological phenomena (Carter et al., 2010; Webb-Davies, 2016), the acoustic data they contain is not always of high enough quality, nor is the corpus large enough, to stand alone as the sole source for development of speech technology. A brief history of Welsh in Argentina is presented below, followed by a discussion of the benefits that Argentinean Welsh data may have on future development of Welsh speech technology.

1.2 Argentinean Welsh

The presence of Welsh in Argentina is due to the mid-19th century efforts of a group of Welsh speakers, led by Michael D. Jones, who sought to establish a Welsh colony away from the influence of the English language and British government (Williams, 1975). In 1865, following an agreement with the government of Argentina, a Welsh colony was established in the Patagonia region of of the country. Today, descendants of the original 200 colonists (and of the several thousand who followed in subsequent years) still maintain the Welsh language and culture in Argentina. Modern Welsh speakers are clustered in two areas of

---

[1] `www.bangor.ac.uk/canolfanbedwyr/`
`technolegau_iaith.php.en`
[2] `http://techiaith.cymru/2016/05/`
`introducing-macsen`

[3] `https://apps.apple.com/bs/app/paldaruo/`
`id840185808`
[4] `https://voice.mozilla.org`
[5] `http://techiaith.cymru/data/corpora/`
`twitter`
[6] `http://corpws.cymru/ceg/`
[7] `http://bangortalk.org.uk/`

Chubut Province, in Dyffryn Camwy on the Atlantic coast, and Cwm Hyfryd to the west.

Although inter-generational transmission of the language waned during the 20th century, revitalization efforts were spurred in 1965, the centennial of the original colony's establishment. The centennial celebration renewed interest in Welsh culture and language, and by the 1990s several language initiatives were established which still exist today. These include Welsh language medium primary schools, annual Eisteddfodau (traditional poetry and song competitions), and an ongoing teacher exchange program with Wales through the Welsh Language Project.[8]

2 Discussion

Argentinean Welsh is spoken by a population that is separated from Wales by more than a century of sparse contact as well as a language barrier (bilingualism with Spanish, rather than English). These factors have almost certainly contributed to linguistic divergence in many aspects of Argentinean Welsh. The most salient of these aspects for the purpose of this paper is divergence in the language's sound system, in the acoustic realization and phonological representation of speech sounds. Previous research on speech recognition of dialect and accent differences has shown that, given a large enough data set, systems trained on multiple dialects perform better than those trained on a single dialect (Rao and Sak, 2017; Li et al., 2018; Yang et al., 2018). Other work has found that including accent classification when training a multi-accent speech recognition system improved later classification of both accent-classified and accent-unclassified datasets (Jain et al., 2018). Before addressing specific evidence for phonetic and phonological differences between Argentinean Welsh and other dialects of Welsh, the next section discusses the reasoning for including dialectal variation in speech technology models.

The results of previous research indicate that the inclusion of dialectal acoustic variation can provide a more variable and more useful data set for the future development of Welsh language technology. I propose that Argentinean Welsh provides a unique opportunity to broaden the language data base from which Welsh speech technologies are developed. Specific aspects of Argentinean Welsh variation, which may be due to synchronic effects from first language Spanish, the effect of lifelong Spanish bilingualism, or diachronic dialect divergence, are discussed below.

Today, all adult speakers of Welsh are at least bilingual, either with English (in Wales) or with Spanish (in Argentina). This situation complicates what might otherwise be a straightforward dialect comparison between differing varieties of Welsh. Cross-linguistic influence from competing languages Spanish and English is entangled with other linguistic pressures, including effects of first language (L1) on second language (L2) speech, and historical language change as a result of contact. Teasing apart these intertwined factors is far beyond the scope of this paper, and it is sufficient for our purposes to acknowledge that multiple factors exist, and that they likely influence the Welsh language in both regions. Recent work has used experimental methods and corpus analyses to investigate the realization of sound contrasts in Argentinean Welsh that are hypothesized to be susceptible to influence from Spanish contact.

Sleeper (2015) investigated the realization of voice onset time (VOT) in the Welsh voiceless stop series /p t k/. It was hypothesized that while contact with the English system reinforces the retention of the Welsh voiceless aspirated-voiceless unaspirated VOT contrast, contact with Spanish in Argentina may have resulted in a shift to a more Spanish-like voiced-voiceless unaspirated system. Sleeper extracted VOT values from word-initial instances of /p t k/ produced in conversational speech by Welsh bilinguals in Argentina and in Wales, recorded in the Patagonia and Siarad corpora (Deuchar et al., 2014). Results confirmed his hypothesis, with Argentinean Welsh-Spanish bilingual speakers producing shorter Spanish-like VOT in voiceless-stop initial Welsh words, compared to the English-like VOT produced by the Welsh-English bilingual group.

Bell (2018) collected productions of Welsh vowels from Welsh-Spanish bilinguals in Argentina and Welsh-English bilinguals in Wales in order to investigate differences in the acoustic realization of allophonic and phonemic vowel length. Because Spanish does not contrast vowels on the basis of length, nor does duration vary allophonically to the extent that it does in Welsh or English, it was hypothesized that Welsh-Spanish bilinguals were

---

[8]https://wales.britishcouncil.org/en/
programmes/education/welsh-language-
project

likely to exhibit differences in their production of long and short Welsh vowels. Results showed that Welsh-Spanish bilinguals produced phonemic vowel length contrasts in much the same way as Welsh-English bilinguals (relying on both vowel duration and spectral quality), but were less similar in production of allophonic duration differences conditioned by following consonant voicing.

Differences in the acoustic realization of the factors mentioned above are likely to prove challenging for an automatic speech recognition system trained only on Welsh produced by fluent speakers in Wales. The differences observed in Argentinean Welsh generally appear to reduce acoustic contrast between Welsh phonemes (the voiceless /p t k/ and voiced /b d ɡ/ stop series, or the vowel length contrast separating minimal pairs such as /mor/ *mor* 'so' and /moːr/ *môr* 'sea'). The collapse of contrasting acoustic cues to these (and potentially other) phonemic differences in Argentinean Welsh is likely to prove challenging for an automatic speech recognition system trained on other dialects of the language.

One solution to this problem, as often seems to be the case in the domain of speech technology, is more data. Natural and lab-produced speech datasets collected from speakers of Argentinean Welsh will serve to diversify the information set from which statistical generalizations about acoustic-phonetic realizations of Welsh are drawn. Knowledge-based approaches to speech recognition that incorporate linguistic generalizations such as phonological rules into the system should also be considered, as they may be well-suited to ASR development from small datasets (Besacier et al., 2006; Gaikwad et al., 2010).

3 Suggestions for future work

While advocating for the inclusion of Argentinean Welsh data in future Welsh speech technology projects is well and good, it must also be acknowledged that there are challenges to doing so. The Welsh-speaking population of Argentina is sparse compared to that of Wales, with speaker numbers in the low thousands, spread throughout the region (Ó Néill, 2005). This problem may be overcome by making use of existing community networks and organizations. Data collection, participant recruitment, and outreach could all potentially be integrated with community events such as the annual Eisteddfod in both the eastern and western Argentinean Welsh communities. Additionally, the Welsh Language Project and Menter Patagonia program involve networks of Welsh language educators in the region who may be interested in integrating speech technology participation into their classrooms of speakers at all levels.

As the resources for Welsh speech technology continue to grow, the opportunity to include data from speakers of Welsh in Argentina increases. Through projects like the speech-collecting Paldaruo app and Mozilla CommonVoice (Prys and Jones, 2018), it is increasingly possible to target and recruit participants who are speakers of Argentinean Welsh (and of course, other minority dialects of the language) through crowdsourcing methods. Encouraging participation in the CommonVoice initiative, which is online and requires little time commitment is a simple first step toward crowdsourcing Argentinean Welsh data.

4 Conclusion

This paper has argued that the dialect of Welsh spoken in Argentina presents a valuable resource for the continuing development of Welsh speech technology. Technologies such as speech recognition benefit from the inclusion of variation (both individual and dialectal) in the data from which they are developed. I have shown that the dialect of Argentinean Welsh is different from other dialects of Welsh in the way speakers acoustically realize underlying phonemic contrasts. This variation, if included in speech technology training data, will serve to develop technologies that will be accessible to more speakers, including those who are less fluent, or who due to language background and L2 cross-linguistic influence are not able to fully take advantage of current Welsh speech technology.

Furthermore, inclusion of the Argentinean Welsh community in the development of Welsh speech technology will strengthen ties between speakers in Wales and Argentina. The goals of Welsh language revitalization programs in both countries include supporting new speakers of the language, and making speech technology accessible and responsive to those new speakers will further progress toward that goal. The Welsh-speaking population of Argentina is a valuable resource, and outreach and integration efforts to and with community members can only stand to benefit future efforts in the development of speech technology for all Welsh speakers.

References

Bell, Elise Adrienne. 2017. Perception of Welsh vowel contrasts by Welsh-Spanish bilinguals in Argentina. In *Linguistic Society of America Annual Meeting*. Linguistic Society of America Annual Meeting.

Bell, Elise Adrienne. 2018. *Perception and Production of Welsh Vowels by Welsh-Spanish Bilinguals*. Ph.D. thesis, The University of Arizona.

Besacier, Laurent, V-B Le, Christian Boitet, and Vincent Berment. 2006. ASR and translation for under-resourced languages. In *2006 IEEE International Conference on Acoustics Speech and Signal Processing Proceedings*, volume 5, pages V–V. IEEE.

Carter, Diana, Peredur Davies, M. Carmen Parafita Couto, and Margaret Deuchar. 2010. A corpus-based analysis of codeswitching patterns in bilingual communities. In *Proceedings: XXIX Simposio Internacional de la Sociedad Española de Lingüística*, volume 1.

Deuchar, Margaret P., Peredur Davies, Jon Russell Herring, M. Carmen Parafita Couto, and D Carter. 2014. Building bilingual corpora. In Thomas, E M and I Mennen, editors, *Advances in the Study of Bilingualism*. Multilingual Matters, Bristol.

Escudero, P. 2009. Linguistic perception of 'similar' L2 sounds. In Boersma, Paul and S. Hamann, editors, *Phonology in perception*, pages 151–190. Mouton de Gruyter, Berlin.

Flege, James E., Ocke-Schwen Bohn, and Sunyoung Jang. 1997. Effects of experience on non-native speakers' production and perception of English vowels. *Journal of Phonetics*, 25:437–470.

Flege, James E., Carlo Schirru, and Ian R.A. MacKay. 2003. Interaction between the native and second language phonetic subsystems. *Speech Communication*, 40:467–491.

Gaikwad, Santosh K, Bharti W Gawali, and Pravin Yannawar. 2010. A review on speech recognition technique. *International Journal of Computer Applications*, 10(3):16–24.

Jain, Abhinav, Minali Upreti, and Preethi Jyothi. 2018. Improved accented speech recognition using accent embeddings and multitask learning. In *Proc. INTERSPEECH. ISCA*.

Jones, Dewi Bryn, Gruffudd Prys, and Delyth Prys. 2016. Vocab: a dictionary plugin for web sites. *PARIS Inalco du 4 au 8 juillet 2016*, page 93.

Jones, Robert Owen. 1984. Change and variation in the Welsh of Gaiman, Chubut. In Ball, Martin J. and Glyn E. Jones, editors, *Welsh phonology*, pages 237–261. University of Wales Press, Cardiff.

Jones, Robert Owen. 1998. The Welsh language in Patagonia. In Jenkins, Geraint H., editor, *A social history of the Welsh language: Language and community in the nineteenth century*, pages 287–316. University of Wales Press, Cardiff.

Li, Bo, Tara N Sainath, Khe Chai Sim, Michiel Bacchiani, Eugene Weinstein, Patrick Nguyen, Zhifeng Chen, Yanghui Wu, and Kanishka Rao. 2018. Multi-dialect speech recognition with a single sequence-to-sequence model. In *2018 IEEE International Conference on Acoustics, Speech and Signal Processing (ICASSP)*, pages 4749–4753. IEEE.

Ó Néill, Diarmui. 2005. *Rebuilding the Celtic languages: reversing language shift in the Celtic countries*. Y Lolfa.

Prys, Delyth and Dewi Bryn Jones. 2015. National language technologies portals for lrls: A case study. In *Language and Technology Conference*, pages 420–429. Springer.

Prys, Delyth and Dewi Bryn Jones. 2018. Gathering data for speech technology in the welsh language: A case study. *Sustaining Knowledge Diversity in the Digital Age*, page 56.

Prys, Delyth, Gruffudd Prys, and Dewi Bryn Jones. 2016. Cysill ar-lein: A corpus of written contemporary welsh compiled from an on-line spelling and grammar checker. In *LREC*.

Rao, Kanishka and Haşim Sak. 2017. Multi-accent speech recognition with hierarchical grapheme based models. In *2017 IEEE international conference on acoustics, speech and signal processing (ICASSP)*, pages 4815–4819. IEEE.

Sleeper, Morgan. 2015. Contact effects on voice-onset time (vot) in patagonian welsh. *Journal of the International Phonetic Association*, pages 1–15.

Webb-Davies, Peredur. 2016. Does the old language endure? Age variation and change in contemporary Welsh grammar. In *Welsh Linguistics Seminar*.

Williams, Glyn. 1975. *The desert and the dream: A study of Welsh colonization in Chubut 1865 – 1915*. University of Wales Press, Cardiff.

Yang, Xuesong, Kartik Audhkhasi, Andrew Rosenberg, Samuel Thomas, Bhuvana Ramabhadran, and Mark Hasegawa-Johnson. 2018. Joint modeling of accents and acoustics for multi-accent speech recognition. In *2018 IEEE International Conference on Acoustics, Speech and Signal Processing (ICASSP)*, pages 1–5. IEEE.

Development of a Universal Dependencies treebank for Welsh

Johannes Heinecke
Orange Labs
2 rue Pierre Marzin
F - 22307 Lannion cedex
`johannes.heinecke@orange.com`

Francis M. Tyers
Department of Linguistics
Indiana University
Bloomington, IN
`ftyers@iu.edu`

Abstract

This paper describes the development of the first syntactically-annotated corpus of Welsh within the Universal Dependencies (UD) project. We explain how the corpus was prepared, and some Welsh-specific constructions that require attention. The treebank currently contains 10 756 tokens. An 10-fold cross evaluation shows that results of both, tagging and dependency parsing, are similar to other treebanks of comparable size, notably the other Celtic language treebanks within the UD project.

1 Introduction

The Welsh Treebank is the third Celtic language within the Universal Dependencies project (Nivre et al., 2016), after Irish (Lynn and Foster, 2016) and Breton (Tyers and Ravishankar, 2018). The main goal of the Universal Dependencies treebanks is to have many different languages annotated with identical guidelines and universally defined set of universal POS tags and dependency relations. These cross-linguistically consistent grammatical annotations can be used, for instance, for typological language comparison or developping and evaluating cross-linguistic tagging and parsing tools.

The motivation was twofold: To have a Welsh treebank annotated using the same guidelines as many existing treebanks which permits language comparison and to have a (start for a) treebank which can be used to train dependency parsers. Since the UD project already contains 146 treebanks for 83 languages and provides annotation principles which have been used in typological very different languages, we chose to develop the Welsh treebank within the UD project. At the time of writing 601 sentences with 10 756 tokens in total have been annotated and released with UD version 2.4.

The paper is laid out as follows: in Section 2 we give a short typological overview of Welsh. Section 3 describes briefly prior work for Welsh in computational linguistics and syntax as well as existing resources. In sections 4 and 5 we describe the annotated corpus, the preprocessing steps and present some particularities of Welsh and how we annotate them. Section 6 explains the validation process. We conclude with a short evaluation in section 7 and some remarks on future work (section 8).

2 Welsh

Welsh is a Celtic language of the Brythonic branch[1] of the Insular Celtic languages. There are about 500 000 (Jones, 2012) native speakers in Wales (United Kingdom). Apart from very young children, all speakers are bilingual with English. There are also a few thousand Welsh speakers in the province of Chubut, in Argentina, who are the descendants of Welsh emigrants of the 1850s, who are now all bilingual with Spanish. A short overview on the Welsh Grammar is given in Thomas (1992) and Thorne (1992), more detailed information can be found in Thorne (1993) and King (2003).

Even though Welsh is a close cognate to Breton (and Cornish), it is different from a typological point of view. Like Breton (and the Celtic languages of the Goidelic branch), it has initial conso-

© 2019 The authors. This article is licensed under a Creative Commons 4.0 licence, no derivative works, attribution, CC-BY-ND.

---

[1]Together with Breton and Cornish

nant mutations, inflected prepositions (*ar* "on", *ar-naf i* "on me"), genitive constructions with a single determiner (*tŷ'r frenhines*, lit. "house the queen": "the house of the queen") and impersonal verb forms. However, unlike Breton, Welsh has a predominantly verb-subject-object (VSO) word order, does not have composed tenses with an auxiliary corresponding to "have" and uses extensively periphrastic verbal clauses to convey tense and aspect (Heinecke, 1999). It has only verbnouns instead of infinitives (direct objects become genitive modifiers or possessives). Like Irish but unlike Breton Welsh does not have a verb "to have" to convery possession. It uses a preposition "with" instead: *Mae dau fachgen gen i* "I have two sons", lit. "There is two son(SG) with me". Another feature of Welsh is the vigesimal number system (at least in the formal registers of the language) and non-contiguous numerals (*tri phlentyn ar hugain* "23 children", lit. "three child(SG) on twenty").

3 Related Work

Welsh has been the object of research in computational linguistics, notably for speech recognition and speech synthesis (Williams, 1999; Williams et al., 2006; Williams and Jones, 2008), as well as spell checking and machine translation. An overview can be found in Heinecke (2005), more detailed information about existing language technology for Welsh is accessible at `http://techiaith.cymru`. Research on Welsh syntax within various frameworks is very rich: Awbery (1976), Rouveret (1990), Sadler (1998), Sadler (1999), Roberts (2004), Borsley et al. (2007), Tallerman (2009), Borsley (2010) to cite a few.

The only available annotated corpus to our knowledge is *Cronfa Electroneg o Gymraeg* (CEG) (Ellis et al., 2001), which contains about one million tokens, annotated with POS and lemmas. The CEG corpus contains texts from novels and short stories, religious texts and non-fictional texts in the fields of education, science, business or leisure activities. It also contains texts from newspapers and magazines and some transcribed spoken Welsh.

Currently work is under way for the National Corpus of Contemporary Welsh[2]. It is a very large corpus which contains spoken and written Welsh. currently the existing data is not annotated in syntax (dependency or other). Members of the CorCenCC project also work on WordNet Cymraeg,

a Welsh version of WordNet. Further corpora (including CEG) are available at University of Bangor's Canolfan Bedwyr [3].

Other important resources are the proceedings of the Third Welsh Assembly[4] and *Eurfa*, a full form dictionary[5] with about 10 000 lemmas (210 578 forms). There is also the full form list for Welsh of the Unimorph project[6]. Currently, however, this list contains only 183 lemmas (10 641 forms).

The Welsh treebank is comparable in size to the Breton treebank (10 348 tokens, 888 sentences). The Irish treebank is twice as big with 23 964 tokens (1 020 sentences). UD treebanks vary very much in size. Currently the largest UD treebank is the German-HDT with 3 055 010 tokens. The smallest is Tagalog with just 292 words. Average size for all treebanks is 150 827 tokens, median size is 43 754 tokens.

4 Corpus

Like every language, Welsh has formal and informal registers. All of those are written, which makes it difficult to constitute a homogeneous corpus. The differences are not only a question of style, but are also of morphological and sometimes of syntactic nature. Usually for the written language distinction is made between Literary Welsh (cf. grammars by Williams (1980) and Thomas (1996)) and Colloquial Welsh (Uned Iaith Genedlaethol (1978)) including an attempted new standard, *Cymraeg Byw* "Living Welsh" (Education Department, 1964; Davies, 1988)). Cymraeg Byw, however, has fallen out of fashion since. For the UD Welsh treebank, we chose sentences of Colloquial written Welsh.

The sentences of the initial version of the treebank have been taken from varying sources, like the Welsh language Wikipedia, mainly from pages on items about Wales, like on the *Urdd Gobaith Cymru*, the *Eisteddfodau* or Welsh places, since it is much more probable that native Welsh speakers contributed to these pages. Other sources for individual sentences were the Welsh Assembly corpus mentioned above, Welsh Grammars (in order to cover syntactic structures less frequently seen) or

---

[2] `http://www.corcencc.org/`

[3] cf.　　Canolfan Bedwyr, University of Bangor, `https://www.bangor.ac.uk/canolfanbedwyr/ymchwil_TI.php.en` and `http://corpws.cymru`

[4] `http://cymraeg.org.uk/kynulliad3/`

[5] `http://eurfa.org.uk/`

[6] `http://www.unimorph.org/`

web sites from Welsh institutions (Welsh Universities, *Cymdeithas yr Iaith*). Finally some sentences origin from Welsh language media (*Y Golwg*, *BBC Cymru*) and blogs. Even though a few of the sentences from Wikipedia may look awkward or incorrect to native speakers, these sentences are the reality of written Welsh and are therefore included in the treebank.

The different registers of Welsh mean, that theoretically "identical" forms may appear in diverging surface representations: so the very formal *yr ydwyf i* "I am" (lit. "(affirmative) am I") can take the following (more or less contracted) forms in written Welsh: *rydwyf (i), rydwi, rydw (i), dwi*. In the treebank, we annotate these forms as multi-token words. For layout reasons, we do not split these forms in all examples in this paper. Where it is the case, we mark multi-token words with a box around the corresponding words. The same applies for the negation particle *ni(d)* which is often contracted with the following form of *bod*, if the latter has an initial vowel: *nid oedd* "(he) was not" > *doedd*. Sometimes dialectal variants appear in the Written language: *oeddan* vs *oedden* "(we) were". The corpus of the Welsh treebank retains the original forms. However, we use standard lemmas (Thomas and Bevan, 1950 2002).

4.1 Preprocessing

In order to initiate and to speed up the annotation process, we transformed the CEG corpus (forms, lemmas and POS) into UD's CoNLL-U format (cf. figure 1) and replaced CEG's part-of-speech tags into UD UPOS. During this step we also corrected annotation errors (notably non-ambiguous cases) and added information about which consonant mutation is present, if any. We then used the *Eurfa* full-form dictionary to enrich the CoNLL-U format with morpho-syntactic features. On this UD compatible Welsh corpus, we trained the UD-pipe tagger and lemmatizer (Straka and Straková, 2017) using word embeddings for Welsh trained on the Welsh Wikipedia with FastText and provided by Bojanowski et al. (2017). With this model we POS-tagged our corpus. A second script pre-annotated some basic dependency relations (`case`- and `det` relations).

In addition to the UD standard, we defined language specific XPOS (table 1), a morphological feature `Mutation` with three values to indicate the consonant mutation, since they carry syntac-

tically relevant information, and some subtypes for dependency relations, also frequently used in other languages: `acl:relcl` (relative clauses) and `flat:name` (flat structures for multi-word named entities).

UPOS	Welsh specific XPOS
ADJ	pos, cmp, eq, ord, sup
ADP	prep, cprep
AUX	aux, impf, ante, post, verbnoun
NOUN	noun, verbnoun
PRON	contr, dep, indp, intr, pron, refl, rel
PROPN	org, person, place, propn, work

Table 1: Welsh specific XPOS

5 Dependencies

The POS-tagged corpus was then manually annotated[7] and all layers were validated: lemmas, UPOS, XPOS (see section 5), and dependency relations using the annotation guidelines of Universal Dependencies. The annotation were made by a single annotator.

The following subsections discuss some of the particularities of the Welsh language, and how these were annotated.

5.1 Nominal genitive construction

Similar to the other Celtic languages, but also to genetically very different languages like Arabic, nominal genitive constructions are juxtaposed nounphrases. Only the last nounphrase can have a determiner (article, possessive), which determines the whole construction (fig. 2).

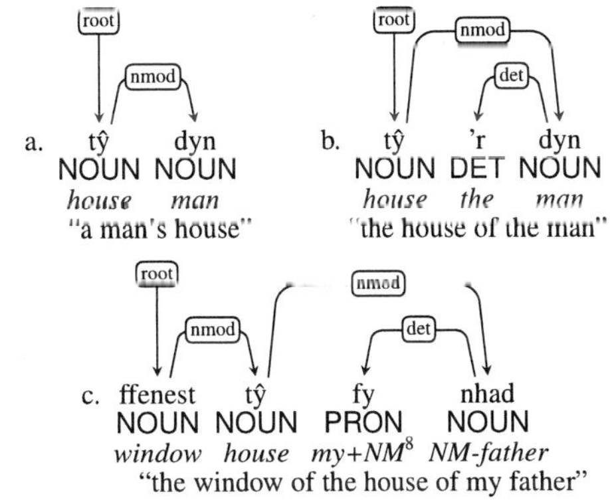

Figure 2: noun phrases

---

[7]using `https://github.com/Orange-OpenSource/conllueditor/`

```
#id form   lemma   UPOS XPOS features                    head deprel enh.deps misc
1   tai    tŷ      NOUN noun Gender=Masc|Number=Plur 0    root   _            SpaceAfter=No
2   'r     y       DET  art  _                       3    det    _            _
3   brenin brenin  NOUN noun Gender=Masc|Number=Sing 1    nmod   _            _
```

Figure 1: CoNLL-U format: Every token is a line of 10 tab-separated columns UPOS are universal POS tags, XPOS are language specific. The enhanced dependencies column adds a second layer of annotation (not used yet in Welsh). The misc column provides information about inter-token spaces, glosses, transcription etc. For details, see `https://universaldependencies.org/format.html`

5.2 Periphrastic verbal construction

The verb can be seen as the central word in dependency syntax. Since the Welsh verb has only two tenses in the indicative mood (Future and Past, both denoting perfective aspect), all other tense and aspect forms are built using periphrastic constructions using one or more forms of the verbnoun *bod* "to be". Whereas inflected verbs (fig. 3) are annotated in a straight forward way, the periphrastic forms need some attention.

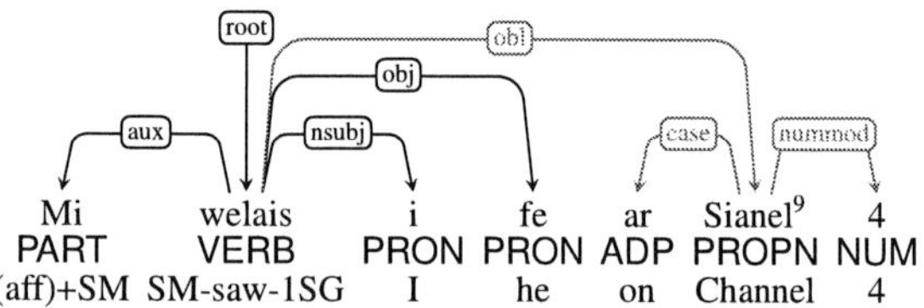

"I saw him on Channel 4"

Figure 3: Inflected verb

As said before, Welsh has no infinitives, but verbnouns, which mark objects differently compared to inflected verbs. Whereas in English a direct object is the same (*I saw **him***; *to see **him***), in Welsh the inflected form uses a different pronoun series (called independent pronouns in Welsh grammar tradition) than the verbnoun. Note that Welsh does not distinguish between subject and object pronouns, but between independent and dependent pronouns. The former are used in subject and object position of inflected verbs, the latter for possessives and "object" relations on verbnouns, e.g. *ei gar* "his car" or mark the direct object for verbnouns *ei gweld* literally "his seeing", e.g. "to see him". For this reason, verbnouns have a different language specific XPOS (verbnoun

---

[8]+NM means that this word triggers soft mutation on the following word, NM- means that this word undergoes nasal mutation. Similarly we use SM and AM for soft and aspirated mutation, respectively. For more details on mutations, see King (2003, pp. 14ff). Some mutations are triggered by syntactic functions and not by a preceding word, e.g. temporal and spatial adverbials or undefinite direct objects.

[9]Dependency relations in gray are irrelevant for the point made in the example.

vs. noun) but the same UPOS (NOUN) as nouns. Other treebanks in the UD project with verbnouns do the same (notably Irish and, in some well defined, cases Polish). The periphrastic construction (fig. 4) employs at least one (inflected) form of *bod* (here *ydw*) and a time or aspect marker (TAM) like *yn* or *wedi* etc. The (independent) pronoun after the verbnoun (VN) is facultative and repeats the (dependent) pronoun before the verbnoun *gweld* (here undergone soft mutated to *weld*).

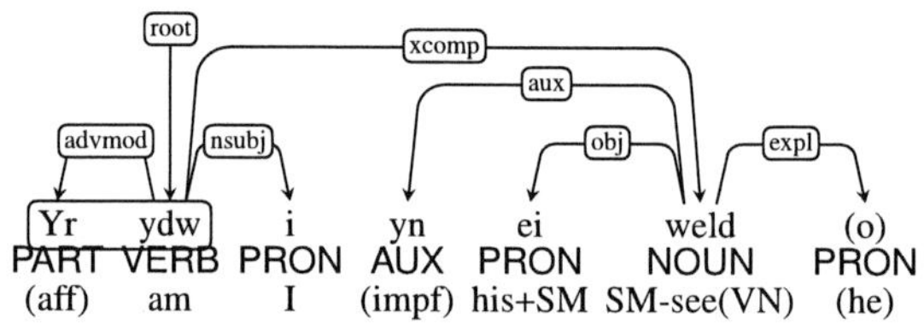

"I am seeing him"
(lit. "I am (impf) his seeing he")

Figure 4: Periphrastic construction

The same annotation can be found in the Irish treebank (fig. 5). In the Breton treebank, however, the infinitive is the phrasal head (6) to which the auxiliary verb is attached as an `aux`.

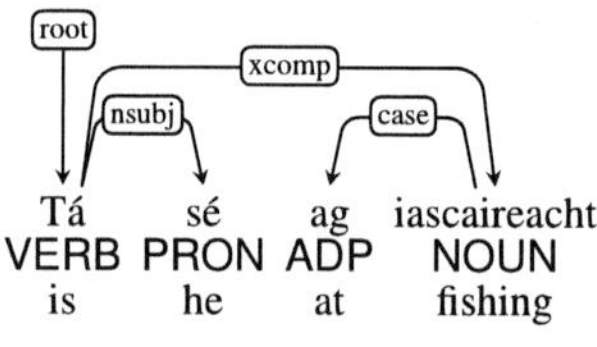

"He is fishing"

Figure 5: Irish periphrastic construction (from UD Irish-IDT:948)

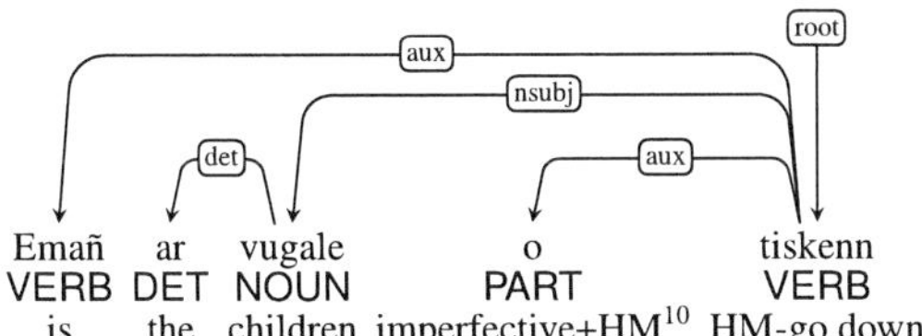

"The children are going down."

Figure 6: Breton periphrastic construction (from UD Breton-KEB:grammar.vislcg.txt:54:1065

Periphrastic constructions can be nested, so to have the imperfective version of figure 4 we get the Sentence shown in figure 7.

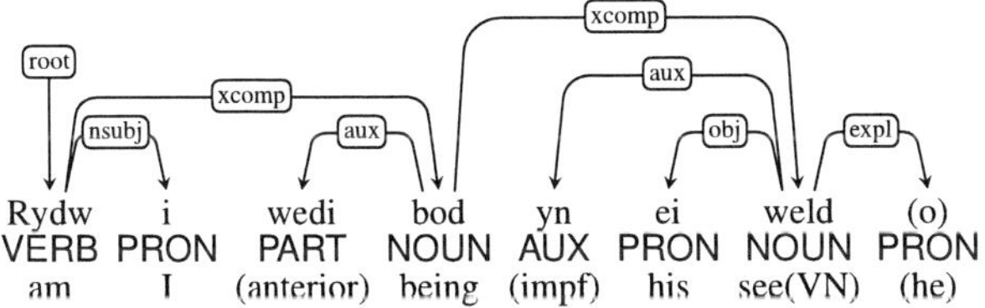

"I have been seeing him"
(lit. "I am after being his seeing he")

Figure 7: Nested periphrastic construction

If a periphrastic phrase is used as a subordinate, even the head (*bod*) is a verbnoun and the subject is marked using the dependent (possessive) pronoun (fig. 8, next page).

In Welsh the main (semantic) time (past, present, future) is nearly always expressed as a form of *bod*. Relative time positions (before or after) are marked using other TAM markers (*ar*, *am* (posteriority, "about to"), *wedi* (anteriority, cf. English Present/Past Perfect), *hen* (distant anteriority), *newydd* (recent anteriority, cf. Heinecke (1999, p. 271)). We have decided to use the inflected form of *bod* as the syntactic head and link the subsequent verbnoun *bod* and finally the verbnoun carrying the meaning with as x comp to avoid completely flat trees which do not show the inherent structure of these phrases.

5.3 Subjects in subordinate phrases

Subordinate phrases very often do not have inflected verbs, but use TAM or prepositions to establish a relative time with respect to the main phrase. In these cases the subject has a case dependant (preposition *i* "to", cf. fig. 9 next page,

[10]HM: Breton hard mutation

where the preposition is inflected and appears as *iddo*).

5.4 Impersonal and *cael*-periphrastics

Like the other Celtic languages Welsh has impersonal forms (which are often translated using passives). In this construction the demoted agent can be expressed using the preposition *gan* "with". As in the Irish and Breton treebanks, the core argument of an Impersonal is marked obj (fig. 10). A periphrastic construction is possible using the verb *cael* "get" (fig. 11).

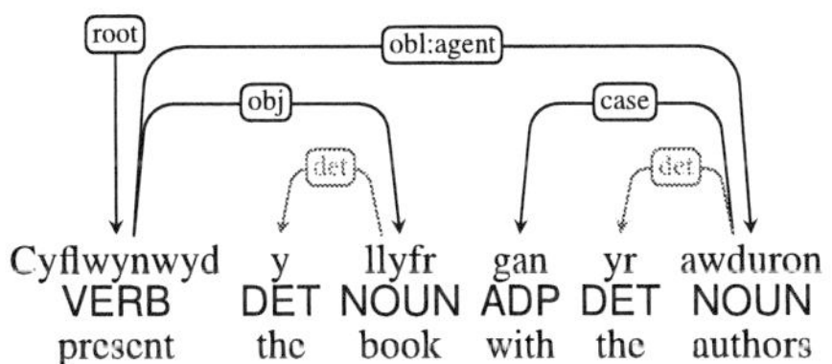

"The book was presented by the authors"
(lit. "One presented the book by the authors")

Figure 10: Impersonal verb form

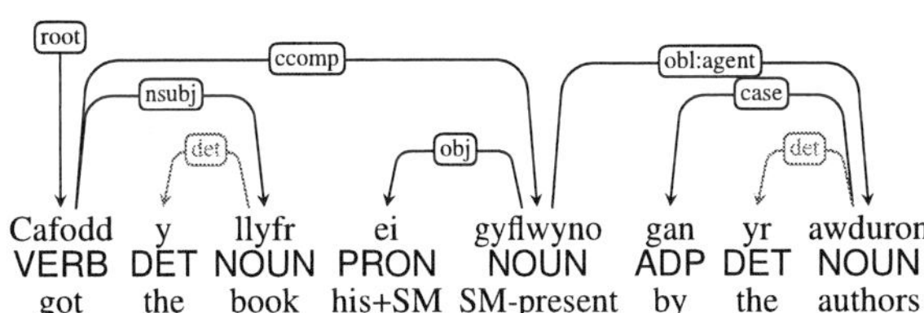

"The book was presented by the authors" (lit. "got the book his presing by the authors")

Figure 11: Periphrastic construction with *cael*

5.5 Nonverbal predicates

Like in most other languages, adjectives and nouns can be head, if they are the predicate. In Welsh, however, such adjectives and nouns need a special predication marker *yn*[11] (fig. 12 and 13).

[11]There are three forms *yn* in Welsh with tree different functions: 1) predicative marker preceding nominal and adjectival predicates, 2) imperfective marker (Isaac, 1994), which precedes a verbnoun (cf. fig. 4), and 3) preposition "in" which triggers nasal mutation. The first two are shortened to *'n* if the preceding word terminates with a vowel.

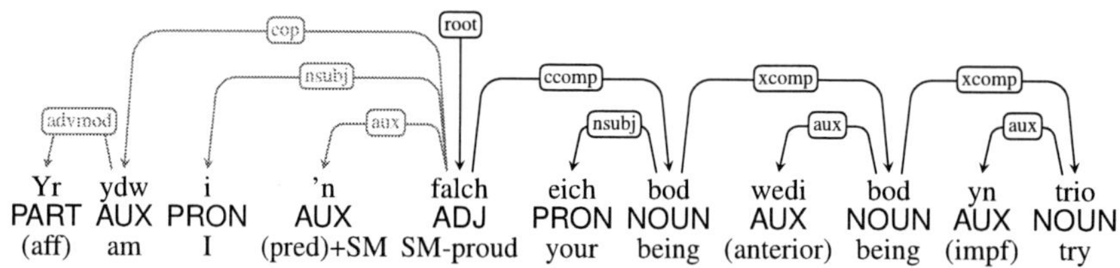

"I'm proud that you have been trying"

Figure 8: Subordinate phrase

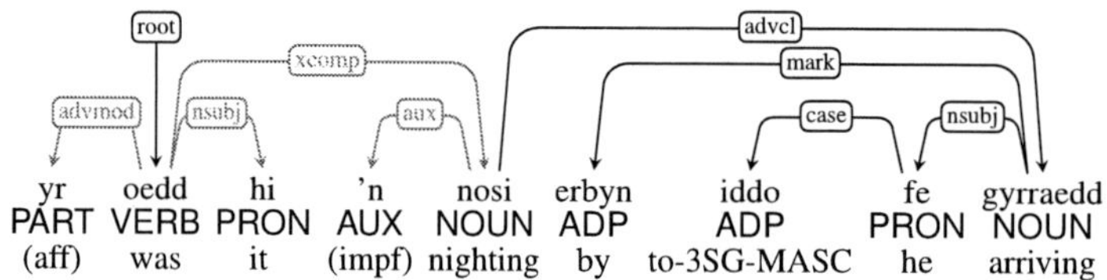

"it was getting dark when he arrived" (lit. "was it nighting, by to-him arrive")

Figure 9: subject in a subordinate phrase

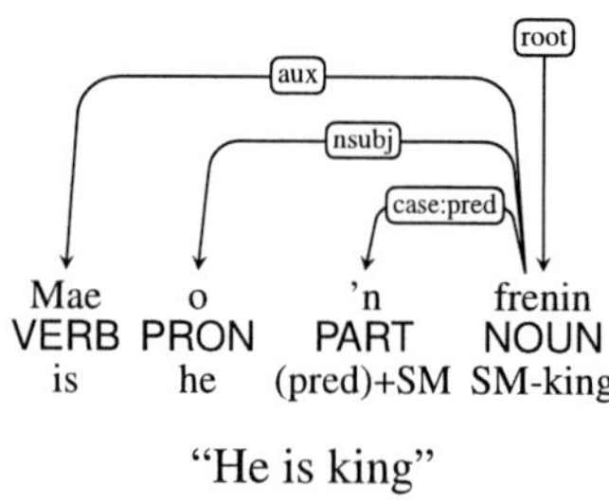

"He is king"

Figure 12: Nonverbal predicates (noun)

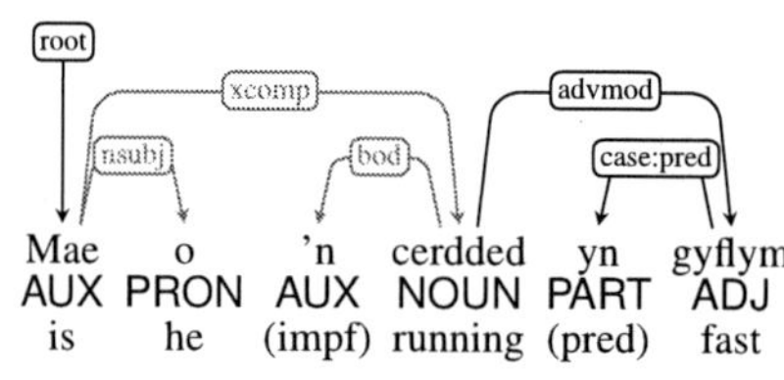

"He is running fast"

Figure 14: adverbial

Since the predicative *yn* is not a preposition[12] but in the same position as a preposition we decided to use the relation `case:pred`.

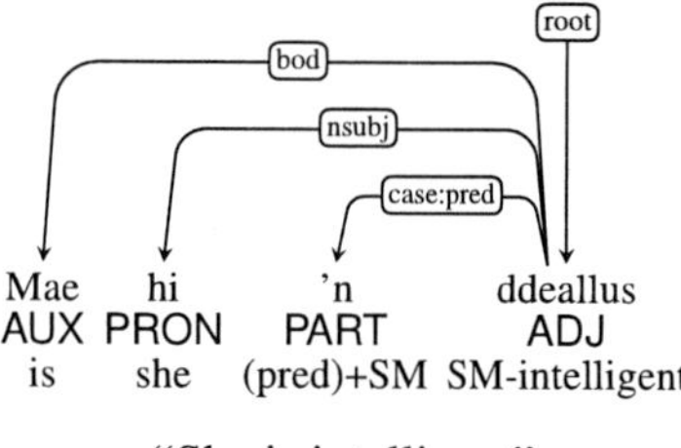

"She is intelligent"

Figure 13: Nonverbal predicates (adjective)

The predication marker *yn* + adjective is also used to have adverbs on verbnouns (fig. 14). In subordinates, the copula *bod* becomes a verbnoun, the subject is attached as possessive using a dependent pronoun (fig. 15, next page).

---

[12]In Welsh dictionaries the predicative *yn* is tagged as an adverb.

5.6 Inflected prepositions

All Celtic languages have contracted forms of prepositions and following pronouns. In Welsh, the pronoun can follow the contracted preposition, so it is more adequate to speak of inflected prepositions instead (Morris-Jones (1913, p. 397), King (2003, p. 268)). This requires a different annotation, since the inflected prepositions (like *gennyt* "with you" in fig. 16) incorporates the `obl` argument. The pronoun "you" is dropped.

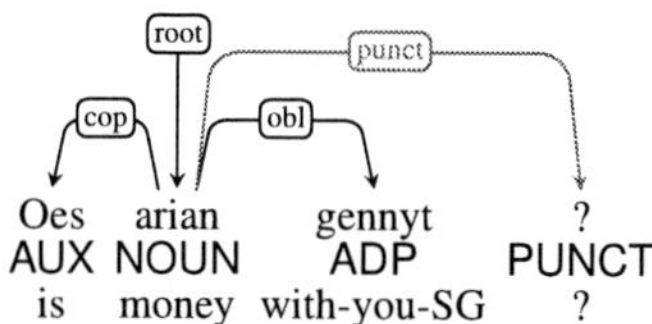

"Do you have money?"

Figure 16: Inflected prepositions (pronoun dropped)

In fig. 17, where the pronoun *ti* is present (`obl`),

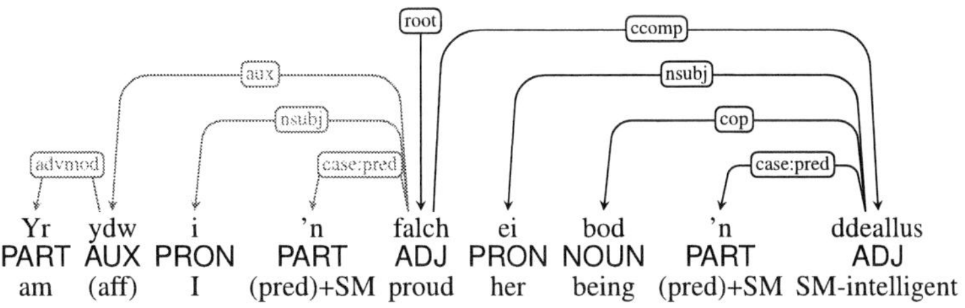

Figure 15: subordinate nonverbal predicate

gennyt is attached as a simple `case` to the pronoun.

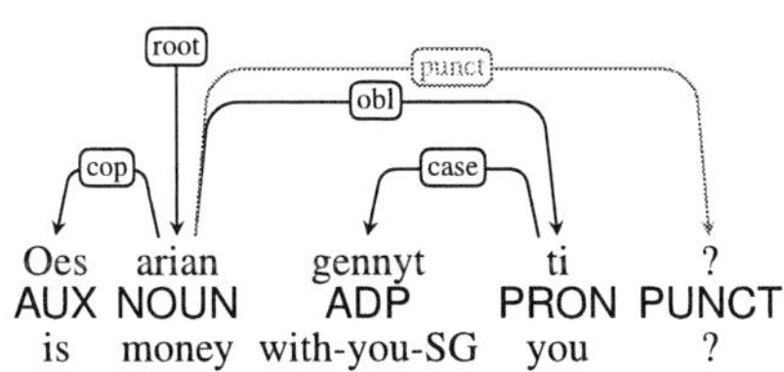

Figure 17: Inflected prepositions (pronoun present)

Using empty nodes and enhanced dependencies, the annotation of an inflected preposition without pronoun becomes more similar to the case with pronoun (fig. 18). The current version of the Welsh treebank is not yet annotated this way.

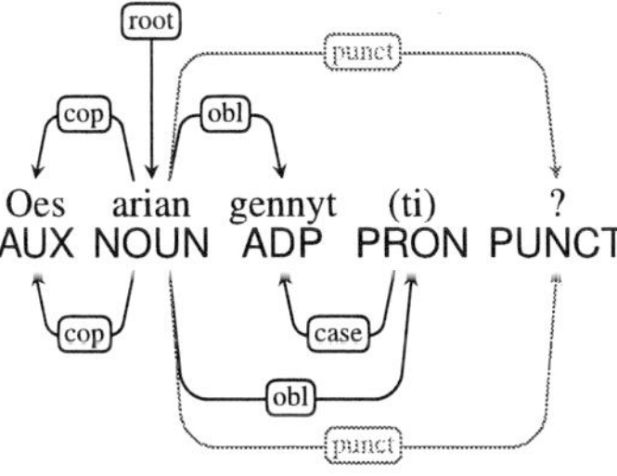

Figure 18: Inflected prepositions with empty words and enhanced dependencies

5.7 Compound numbers

The traditional Welsh numbering is based on a vigesimal number system (20 = *ugain*, 30 = *deg ar hugain* "ten on twenty", 40 = *deugain* "two twenties", 60 = *trigain* "three twenties"). Notably for compound numbers, the counted item comes between the units and the tens of the number, in both cardinals (fig. 19, nouns are always in singular after a numeral) and ordinals (fig. 20).

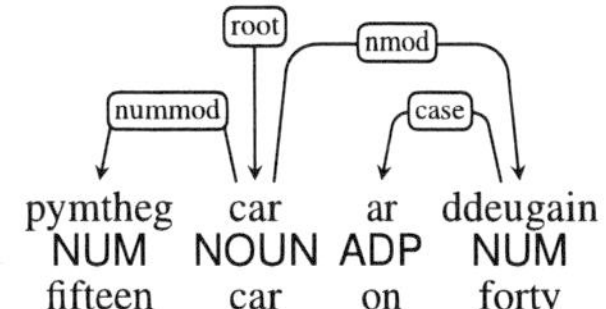

Figure 19: Compound numbers (cardinals)

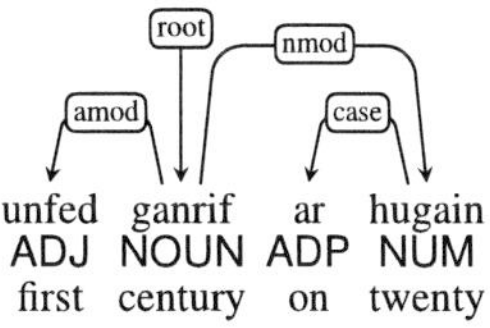

Figure 20: Compound numbers (ordinals)

Breton and Irish use(d) a similar system. There is one example in the Breton UD treebank (fig. 21), which is annotated in a similar way apart from the fact, that Breton uses coordination to join numbers instead of a preposition, as Welsh does). Irish dialects traditionally have a similar structure, even though none is attested in the UD treebank: *dhá bhád is ceithre fichid* "82 boats" (lit. "two boat(sg) and four twenty").

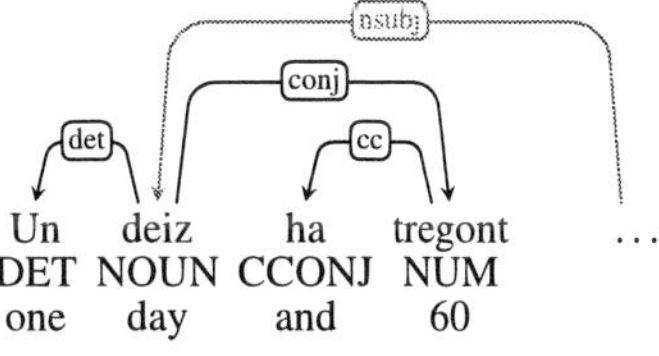

Figure 21: Compound numbers in Breton (from UD Breton-KEB, wikipedia.vislcg.txt:112:3736)

6 Validation

After having all sentences annotated, a post-validation script checked some semantic aspects like the XPOS of inflected prepositions, TAM markers, preverbal particles and consonant mutations (adding the corresponding feature) and looked for potential errors (e.g. a det with a VERB head). This script also checked all forms of the verb *bod* and completed morphological features. For nouns and adjectives the script gives an alert if it cannot determine number (on the base of regular suffixes etc.). The final step is the validation script provided by the UD project which finds formal errors (e.g. dependants on words with a case or aux relation).

Currently the Welsh treebank contains 601 sentences with 10 756 tokens (including punctuation). The average sentence length is 17,9 tokens (shortest sentence: 4 tokens, longest sentence: 59 tokens, median length: 16 tokens). Since verbnouns have the UPOS NOUN, 30.1% of all UPOS are NOUN (table 2).

UPOS	%	XPOS	%
NOUN	30.1	noun	21.3
ADP	12.9	prep	12.4
PUNCT	9.7	punct	9.7
ADJ	6.9	verbnoun	9.1
DET	6.5	art	6.5
PRON	6.3	verb	6.3
VERB	6.3	adj	6.0
AUX	5.9	cconj	2.9
PART	4.4	dep	2.7
PROPN	3.7	impf	2.5
CCONJ	2.9	indep	2.3
ADV	1.9	pred	2.1
NUM	1.3	aux	1.9
		adv	1.9

Table 2: relative frequency of (some) UPOS, XPOS

The relatively small number of tokens with UPOS VERB is due to the fact that verbnouns have the UPOS NOUN. This is relativized if we regard the distribution of the XPOS: noun 21.3%, verbnoun 9.1% + verb 6.3% = 15.4% "verbs".

Table 3 shows all 34 dependency relations used in the Welsh treebank including their frequency. 6 out of the 37 dependency relations proposed[13]

[13]https://universaldependencies.org/u/dep/all.html

deprel	%	deprel	%
case	10.5	ccomp	1.7
punct	9.7	nmod:poss	1.7
nmod	8.4	acl	1.6
det	6.9	advcl	1.4
obl	6.0	acl:relcl	1.2
nsubj	5.7	flat:name	0.8
root	5.6	flat	0.6
obj	5.2	nummod	0.6
advmod	5.2	fixed	0.5
amod	4.8	appos	0.5
xcomp	4.3	expl	0.2
aux	3.7	obl:agent	0.2
conj	3.2	parataxis	0.2
cc	2.9	csubj	0.1
case:pred	2.1	nmod:agent	0.1
mark	2.1	compound	< 0.1
cop	2.0	iobj	< 0.1

Table 3: relative frequency of all 34 used deprels

by the UD guidelines are not used. These are clf used for classifiers (absent in Welsh), orphan (used to annotate ellipses), discourse (interjections) goeswith and reparandum used to correct errors in spelling or tokenization (currently all sentences in the treebank are correctly tokenised) and dep, the default label, if no more specific relation can be chosen).

7 Evaluation

Even though the treebank currently contains only 601 sentences, tests for tagging and dependency parsing (table 6) show results comparable with similar sized treebanks (Tyers and Ravishankar (2018) report a LAS between 64.14% and 74.29% for the Breton treebank, Zeman et al. (2018) mention a LAS of 70.88 for Irish). We used Udpipe (v2, single model for tagging and parsing). Tests with Wikipedia embeddings (500 dimensions) trained with fastText (Bojanowski et al., 2017) did not improve the parsing. This might be caused by the relatively small corpus on which the embeddings have been trained (the Welsh Wikipedia (April 2019) contains only 62MB of compressed raw data (104 000 pages).

For the evaluation we split the 601 sentences into training (80%), dev (10%) and test (10%) corpora and performed a 10-fold cross evaluation. We used the official CoNLL-2018 evaluation script[14]

[14]https://universaldependencies.org/

to calculate all scores. Table 4 shows the results of POS tagging and lemmatisation without and with the Eurfa dictionary, and table 5 the results per UPOS.

	UPOS	XPOS	Lemma
baseline	89.2	87.3	86.7
+Eurfa	87.9	87.5	93.5

Table 4: results of POS tagging and lemmatisation (F-measure

Nearly half of the word forms in the test corpus are out-of-vocabulary (OOV) with respect to the training corpus. The dictionary provided roughly half of the missing words. Thus a quarter of the words in the test corpus remains OOV, which may explain the unexpected low performance (UDpipe switches off its guesser, if a dictionary is provided).

The results of dependency analysis are presented in table 6 using 3 of the standard metrics for dependency parsing (Nivre and Fang, 2017), Labelled Attachment Score (LAS, evaluates heads and dependency labels) or Content Word LAS (CLAS, as LAS, but only for dependency relations of content words (excluding `aux`, `cop`, `mark`, `det`, `clf`, `case`, `cc`).

We run four tests, a model trained solely on the treebank, with dependencies parsed on the results of the tagger, and dependencies parsed using gold tags. The other two tests use the Eurfa dictionary again. The better results of tagging with the full form lexicon, also improves the dependency parsing, if the parsing is done on predicted POS tags. All three metrics increase accordingly.

	POS tags	UAS	LAS	CLAS
baseline	predicted	74.3	63.9	54.8
	gold	82.2	76.2	69.6
+Eurfa	predicted	75.5	64.3	55.4
	gold	81.9	75.9	69.3

Table 6: results of dependency parsing

8 Future Work

The most obvious work is to increase the number of sentences annotated. The current 601 sentences may be a start, but do not cover enough examples to train a robust dependency parser. Another important problem is the absence of very formal

---

```
conll18/conll18_ud_eval.py
```

Welsh (as in the Bible (in its 1588 translation) and some literary works) and of very informal written Welsh (as is used by some Welsh bloggers). Since Welsh is not one of the most widely learned languages, we plan adding glosses and translations to the existing sentences.

With word embeddings becoming more important, work on Welsh word embeddings is needed too. We need to dig into cross-lingual approaches too (e.g. with BERT, (Lample and Conneau, 2019) or UDify (Kondratyuk, 2019)) and/or provide much larger Welsh text corpora than Wikipedia to train word embeddings.

References

Awbery, Gwenllian M. 1976. *The Syntax of Welsh. A transformational Study of The Passive.* Cambridge University Press, Cambridge.

Bojanowski, Piotr, Edouard Grave, Armand Joulin, and Tomas Mikolov. 2017. Enriching Word Vectors with Subword Information. *Transactions of the Association for Computational Linguistics*, 5:135–146.

Borsley, Robert D., Taggie Tallerman, and David Willis. 2007. *The Syntax of Welsh.* Cambridge University Press, Cambridge.

Borsley, Robert D. 2010. An HPSG Approach to Welsh Unbounded Dependencies. In Müller, Stefan, editor, *Proceedings of the 17th International Conference on Head-Driven Phrase Structure Grammar*, pages 80–100, Stanford. CSLI Publications.

Davies, Cennard. 1988. Cymraeg Byw. In Ball, Martin J., editor, *The Use of the Welsh*, pages 200–210. Multilingual Matters, Clevedon.

Education Department, University College of Swansea. 1964. *Cymraeg Byw I.* Llyfrau'r Dryw.

Ellis, Nick C., Cathair O'Dochartaigh, William Hicks, Menna Morgan, and Nadine Laporte. 2001. Cronfa Electroneg o Gymraeg (CEG). A 1 million word lexical database and frequency count for Welsh. `http://www.bangor.ac.uk/ar/cb/ceg.php.en`.

Heinecke, Johannes. 1999. *Temporal Deixis in Welsh and Breton.* Anglistische Forschungen 272. Winter, Heidelberg.

Heinecke, Johannes. 2005. Aspects du traitement automatique du gallois. In *Actes de TALN 2005. Atelier "langues peu dotées"*. ATALA.

Isaac, Graham R. 1994. The Progressive Aspect Marker: W "yn" / OIr. "oc". *Journal of Celtic Linguistics*, 3:33–39.

	baseline			+*Eurfa*		
	precision	recall	f-measure	precision	recall	f-measure
ADJ	82.0	80.5	81.1	92.2	55.9	69.4
ADP	90.6	93.4	91.9	91.2	93.2	92.2
ADV	76.3	76.4	76.0	94.5	74.1	82.9
AUX	81.5	80.3	80.8	76.6	70.1	73.0
CCONJ	84.8	91.8	88.1	88.4	92.3	90.2
DET	97.6	99.0	98.3	98.8	98.0	98.4
NOUN	89.8	91.0	90.4	82.6	97.1	89.2
NUM	89.5	90.3	89.5	96.8	88.0	91.6
PART	88.2	85.3	86.6	79.4	82.5	80.8
PRON	93.8	89.8	91.7	98.5	90.9	94.5
PROPN	75.1	63.0	68.0	92.9	48.4	62.7
PUNCT	99.9	100.0	100.0	99.9	100.0	100.0
SCONJ	89.6	87.0	87.1	97.5	75.1	84.4
SYM	66.7	66.7	66.7	33.3	33.3	33.3
VERB	82.9	83.6	83.1	80.2	83.9	81.8

Table 5: results of POS tagging and lemmatisation per UPOS

Jones, Hywel M. 2012. *A statistical overview of the Welsh language*. Bwrdd yr Iaith Gymraeg/Welsh Language Board, Cardiff.

King, Gareth. 2003. *Modern Welsh. A comprehensive grammar*. Routledge, London, New York, 2 edition.

Kondratyuk, Daniel. 2019. 75 Languages, 1 Model: Parsing Universal Dependencies Universally. http://arxiv.org/abs/1904.02099.

Lample, Guillaume and Alexis Conneau. 2019. Cross-lingual Language Model Pretraining. http://arxiv.org/abs/1901.07291.

Lynn, Teresa and Jennifer Foster. 2016. Universal Dependencies for Irish. In *CLTW*, Paris.

Morris-Jones, John. 1913. *A Welsh Grammar. Historical and Comparative*. Clarendon Press, Oxford.

Nivre, Joakim and Chiao-Ting Fang. 2017. Universal Dependency Evaluation. In Marneffe, Marie-Catherine de, Joakim Nivre, and Sebastian Schuster, editors, *Proceedings of the NoDaLiDa 2017 Workshop on Universal Dependencies*, pages 86–95, Göteborg.

Nivre, Joakim, Marie-Catherine de Marneffe, Filip Ginter, Yoav Goldberg, Yoav Goldberg, Jan Hajič, Manning Christopher D., Ryan McDonald, Slav Petrov, Sampo Pyysalo, Natalia Silveira, Reut Tsarfaty, and Daniel Zeman. 2016. Universal Dependencies v1: A Multilingual Treebank Collection. In *the tenth international conference on Language Resources and Evaluation*, pages 23–38, Portorož, Slovenia. European Language Resources Association.

Roberts, Ian G. 2004. *Principles and Parameters in a VSO Language. A Case Study in Welsh*. Oxford Studies in Comparative Syntax. Oxford University Press, Oxford.

Rouveret, Alain. 1990. X-Bar Theory, Minimality, and Barrierhood in Welsh. In Randall, Hendryck, editor, *The Syntax of the Modern Celtic Languages*, Syntax and Semantics 23, pages 27–77. Academic Press, New York.

Sadler, Louisa. 1998. Welsh NPs without Head Movement. In Butt, Miriam and Tracy Holloway King, editors, *Proceedings of the LFG98 Conference*, Stanford. CSLI Publications.

Sadler, Louisa. 1999. Non-Distributive Features in Welsh Coordination. In Butt, Miriam and Tracy Holloway King, editors, *Proceedings of the LFG99 Conference*. CSLI Publications, Stanford.

Straka, Milan and Jana Straková. 2017. Tokenizing, POS Tagging, Lemmatizing and Parsing UD 2.0 with UDPipe. In *ACL 2017*, pages 88–99, Vancouver.

Tallerman, Maggie. 2009. Phrase structure vs. dependency: The analysis of Welsh syntactic soft mutation. *Journal of Linguistics*, 45(1):167–201.

Thomas, R. J. and Gareth A. Bevan. 1950-2002. *Geiriadur Prifysgol Cymru. A Dictionary of the Welsh Language*. Gwasg Prifysgol Cymru, Caerdydd.

Thomas, Alan R. 1992. The Welsh Language. In MacAulay, Donald, editor, *The Celtic languages*, Cambridge language surveys. Cambridge University Press, Cambridge.

Thomas, Peter Wynn. 1996. *Gramadeg y Gymraeg*. Gwasg Prifysgol Cymru, Caerdydd.

Thorne, David. 1992. The Welsh Language, its History and Structure. In Price, Glanville, editor, *The Celtic Connection*, pages 171–205. Colin Smythe, Gerrards Cross.

Thorne, David. 1993. *A Comprehensive Welsh Grammar*. Blackwell, Oxford.

Tyers, Francis M. and Vinit Ravishankar. 2018. A prototype dependency treebank for Breton. In *Traitement Automatique des Langues Naturelles (TALN)*, pages 197–204, Rennes.

Uned Iaith Genedlaethol. 1978. *Gramadeg Cymraeg Cyfoes. Contemporary Welsh Grammar*. Brown a'i Feibion, Y Bontfaen.

Williams, Briony and Rhys James Jones. 2008. Acquiring Pronunciation Data for a Placenames Lexicon in a Less-Resourced Language. In *The sixth international conference on Language Resources and Evaluation*, Marrakech, Maroc. European Language Resources Association.

Williams, Briony, Rhys James Jones, and Ivan Uemlianin. 2006. Tools and resources for speech synthesis arising from a Welsh TTS project. In *The fifth international conference on Language Resources and Evaluation*, Genoa, Italy.

Williams, Stephen Joseph. 1980. *Elements of a Welsh Grammar*. University of Wales Press, Cardiff.

Williams, Briony. 1999. A Welsh speech database. Preliminary result. In *EuroSpeech 1999. Proceedings of the Sixth European Conference on Speech Communication and Technology, Budapest, Hungary, September 5-9, 1999*, Budapest.

Zeman, Daniel, Jan Hajič, Martin Popel, Martin Potthast, Milan Straka, Filip Ginter, Joakim Nivre, and Slav Petrov. 2018. CoNLL 2018 Shared Task: Multilingual Parsing from Raw Text to Universal Dependencies. In Zeman, Daniel and Jan Hajič, editors, *Proceedings of the CoNLL 2018 Shared Task: Multilingual Parsing from Raw Text to Universal Dependencies*, pages 1–21, Brussels. Association for Computational Linguistics.

Code-switching in Irish tweets: A preliminary analysis

Teresa Lynn
ADAPT Centre, School of Computing
Dublin City University
Ireland
teresa.lynn@adaptcentre.ie

Kevin Scannell
Department of Computer Science
Saint Louis University
Missouri, USA
kscanne@gmail.com

Abstract

As is the case with many languages, research into code-switching in Modern Irish has, until recently, mainly been focused on the spoken language. Online user-generated content (UGC) is less restrictive than traditional written text, allowing for code-switching, and as such, provides a new platform for text-based research in this field of study. This paper reports on the annotation of (English) code-switching in a corpus of 1496 Irish tweets and provides a computational analysis of the nature of code-switching amongst Irish-speaking Twitter users, with a view to providing a basis for future linguistic and socio-linguistic studies.

1 Introduction

User-generated content (UGC) provides an insight into the use of language in an informal setting in a way that previously was not possible. That is to say that in the pre-internet era (where most published content was curated and edited), text that was available for analysis was not necessarily reflective of everyday language use. User-generated content, on the other hand, provides a clearer snapshot of a living language in natural, everyday use.

Analysis of minority language UGC in particular provides much insight into the evolution of these languages in the digital age. In some bilingual environments, the overwhelming dominance of a majority language can sometimes restrict and discourage the natural use of a minority language.

Online environments, on the other hand, can offer a kind of 'safe space' in which these languages can co-exist and the minority language can thrive. Additionally, various interesting linguistic phenomena occur online that may be frowned upon in more formal settings. The present paper aims to investigate one such phenomenon among Irish-speaking users of the micro-blogging platform Twitter.

Code-switching occurs whenever a speaker switches between two (or more) languages in a multilingual environment. Negative attitudes towards code-switching have been documented widely in this field – in particular earlier beliefs that code-switching indicated a communicative deficiency or lack of mastery of either language. In fact, the phenomenon is now understood to be indicative of bilingual proficiency (Grosjean, 2010).

Solorio and Liu (2008) note that "when the country has more than one official language, we can find instances of code-switching". Given that Irish is the first official language of the Republic of Ireland, with English as the second,[1] and given the well-known existence of code-switching in the spoken Irish of the Gaeltacht regions (Hickey, 2009), it is unsurprising that Lynn et al. (2015) and Caulfield (2013, p. 208ff) report that code-switching is a common feature in Irish UGC. Our earlier work (Lynn et al., 2015), however, focused only on a part-of-speech (POS) tagging analysis of an Irish Twitter data set, without further exploration of the code-switching phenomenon that was observed. In fact, the English (code-switched) segments of tweets were given a general tag that

---

[1]Note that English is the more dominant language, with only 17.4% of the population reporting use of Irish outside the education system http://www.cso.ie/en/media/csoie/releasespublications/documents/population/2017/7._The_Irish_language.pdf

© 2019 The authors. This article is licensed under a Creative Commons 4.0 licence, no derivative works, attribution, CC-BY-ND.

was also used to label abbreviations, items, out-of-vocabulary (OOV) tokens and other (non-English) foreign words.

Our current study is a continuation of our earlier work. We annotate, document, and analyse the specific nature of code-switching between English and Irish in our corpus of Irish language tweets (Lynn et al., 2015). With this we provide a basis for linguistic research into the way in which Ireland's official languages interact in an online social context. Our contributions are as follows: (i) an enhancement of the POS-tagged Twitter corpus in which English code-switched segments are annotated, (ii) a categorisation of the types of code-switching present in Irish tweets, and (iii) a quantitative report as to the relative frequency and use of English within Irish tweets.

2 Background and Related Work

2.1 Code-switching

Code-switching has been a focus of study for many years, particularly in the area of bilingualism (e.g. Espinosa (1917) and Muysken (1995)). Despite being an early topic of study in the field of computational linguistics (e.g. Joshi (1982)), interest in the computational study of code-switching has grown substantially in recent years with the increased availability of online UGC (Solorio et al., 2014; Molina et al., 2016). This area of study is applicable to many facets of natural language processing (NLP), including automatic language identification (Rosner and Farrugia, 2007) and POS tagging (Solorio and Liu, 2008), for example. In fact, Minocha and Tyers (2014) carried out some preliminary analysis on English-Irish code-switching in the context of automatic language identification. It is worth noting that the advances in the area of NLP for UGC represent a valuable contribution to the field of sociolinguistics, as NLP allows for easier and more efficient processing of large data sets than traditional manual methods (e.g. Nguyen et al. (2016))

There is much debate in the literature about whether the correct umbrella term is *code-switching* or *code-mixing*, or in fact whether both refer to specific types of switching depending on where in the sentence it occurs. In our work, we use the term *code-switching* to cover all instances of the linguistic phenomenon that results in mixed-language text. We divide the instances of code-switching in Irish tweets into four main types:

Inter-sentential: where the switch occurs at a sentence or clause boundary:

(1) *Má tá AON Gaeilge agat, úsáid í! It's Irish Language Week.*
'If you speak ANY Irish, use it! It's Irish Language Week.'

Intra-sentential: where the switch occurs within a sentence or clause:

(2) *Ceol álainn ar @johncreedon on @RTERadio1 now.*
'Lovely music on @johncreedon on @RTERadio1 now.'

Word-level alternation: where the switch occurs within a word:

(3) *Bhfuil do kid ag **mixáil** Gaeilge agus English?*
'Is your kid **mixing** Irish and English?'

Bilingual text is, strictly-speaking, a special case of inter-sentential code-switching, in which the same content is provided in both languages in a single tweet. This is typical on Twitter for users whose followers can be divided into two groups – Irish speakers and non-Irish speakers.[2] Bilingual tweeting aims to be inclusive of a wider audience along with assisting learners in reading the Irish content. Due to the prevalence and importance of such examples, they are given special annotations in the resources described below.

(4) *Happy St Patrick's Day! La Fhéile Pádraig sona daoibh!*

2.2 Code-switching in Irish

Until recently, investigation into the use of code-switching in Irish has focused mainly on transcribed speech. In recent work, Ní Laoire (2016) noted that "[code-switching] has been underrepresented in Irish language corpora and in linguistic and dialectological description and analysis of Irish". In fact, much of the existing literature in this domain focuses on the impact of English as a dominant language in a bilingual environment (e.g. Stenson (1993)), in the context of raising concerns for the survival of the Irish language. In

---

[2]Stenson (1993) refers to the ability of all Irish speakers to speak English as "Universal Bilingualism"

the same vein, Hickey (2009) looks at the contrast between code-switching and borrowing, and its potential prevalence amongst the next generation of native Irish speakers. Her study focuses on such occurrences in unscripted speech of leaders of Irish-language pre-schools in Irish-speaking communities. Atkinson and Kelly-Holmes (2011) also investigate the nature of code-switching in spoken Irish and took a slightly different angle by looking at the use of English-Irish code-switching in comedy – with respect to the relationship between identity and language.

In terms of written text, Bannett Kastor (2008) provides a summary of the few examples of code-switching in Irish literature from the 17th-20th century, which in many cases incidentally can also be noted as being a conduit for comedy.[3] She notes that "multiliterate texts are constructed deliberately so that switch points or other points of linguistic contact within the text often signal additional, metaphorical levels of meaning which are coherent with the theme and/or other aspects of the work." However, such deliberate and planned code-switching differs from the nature of the switching behaviour we are concerned with here.

Interestingly, while code-switching is sometimes regarded in Ireland today (often negatively) as a 'modern' feature of the language, a number of studies have reported on the prevalence of Latin code-switching in Medieval Irish manuscripts, reflecting the multilingual environment in which medieval Irish monks and scribes worked (Dumville, 1990; Müller, 1999; Stam, 2017). These studies highlight code-switching as a natural feature of language use and as a linguistic activity that has continued across generations and across radically different linguistic environments. In the most recent study, Stam (2017) remarks, a propos of the current study, that "it appears that code-switching in writing and in speech are in some ways comparable, especially in informal textual genres". In our current study, we bridge several centuries from the analysis of medieval Irish-Latin code-switching to analyse and process Irish-English code-switching as it is used by today's Irish language community online.

2.3   Irish language on social media

Despite a relatively small population of speakers, the Irish language has a strong online presence on social media platforms such as Facebook, YouTube, Instagram, Snapchat, and Twitter (Lackaff and Moner, 2016). In fact, according to the Indigenous Tweets website, which curates tweets from indigenous and minority languages worldwide, there have been over 3 million tweets sent in Irish to date.[4] With the increased availability of user-generated Irish language content, it is unsurprising that there has been an increased interest in the application of technology to analyse Irish language use online, in order to gain insights into how the language is used (e.g. POS-tagging (Lynn et al., 2015), machine translation (Dowling et al., 2017) and sentiment analysis (Afli et al., 2017)).

3   Code-switching annotation

Of course, in order to carry out an in-depth analysis of the nature of code-switching amongst Irish speakers, sufficient data – in terms of quantity and richness of annotation – must be made available. Such data generally comes in two main forms. One is text that is based on recorded and transcribed speech. In terms of recorded speech, one is more likely to find instances of code-switching in spoken content that is spontaneous and non-scripted (such as the data that was used for an earlier Irish code-switching analysis by Ní Laoire (2016)). Another similarly unedited source is uncurated text such as that found in UGC, which is more likely to contain natural examples of code-switching than standard, well-curated text. In the following section, we describe the creation of our data set of tweets, which we have annotated for code-switching.

3.1   Data Set

Our starting point is the gold standard POS-tagged corpus of 1537 Irish language tweets from our earlier study (Lynn et al., 2015), which sought to provide a basis for NLP analysis of the use of the Irish language online.[5]

For this current study, we review the tags previously assigned to English tokens. In the initial corpus development, English tokens were assigned

---

[3]The data studied came from Irish language poetry, drama, fiction and nonfiction.

[4]`http://indigenoustweets.com`, figures as of July 2019.

[5]Please refer to cited paper for details concerning the POS tagset for Irish tweets.

the catch-all tag 'G' ('general'), which is also used to label other foreign words (of which there are a few, e.g. Japanese), items, and abbreviations. We refine this annotation by now annotating English tokens separately.

Annotation takes place at three levels: (i) `Irish part-of-speech tag level:` The POS-tag is changed from 'G' to 'EN' for all English tokens. (ii) `Code-switching tag level:` The types of code-switching that are present (if any). As per our description in Section 2.1, these labels include INTRA (intra-sentential), INTER (inter-sentential), INTER-BI (bilingualism for the purposes of providing one message in both languages) and WORD (where the word contains code-switched morphemes). (iii) `English part-of-speech tag level:` The INTRA tags have been extended to identify the English POS (e.g. INTRA-V, INTRA-O, etc). These tags are explained in more detail in Table 1.

During annotation, we identified 41 tweets in the Lynn et al. (2015) corpus that contain both English and Irish words, but for which English was the matrix language. This type of issue often can arise within the context of language identification of tweets that contain instances of code-switching. As our interest is in English code-switching within otherwise-Irish language tweets, we have taken the viewpoint that these are errors in language identification, and have removed these examples from the corpus.

(5) *I added a video to a @YouTube playlist <URL>Sharon Shannon - Geantraí na Nollag 2008 - 25-12-08 <URL>*

(6) *Nuacht is déanaí - Twitter Competition - Help us Reach 20K!*

This leaves us with a data set of 1496 tweets annotated with POS and the above-mentioned code-switching tags.

4 Analysis

4.1 Tag distributions

We observe that 254 (16%) of the tweets in the data set contain some form of code-switching. Firstly, it is worth looking at the POS tag distribution across all POS tags in our data:

INTER 412 tokens (representing 43% of the English tokens) are used in an inter-sentential manner – that is, as strings of English that form separate phrases or sentences.

```
LOL       LOL       G
-         -         ,
tell      tell      EN    INTER
ya        ya        EN    INTER
what      what      EN    INTER
-         -         ,
más       má        &
féidir    féidir    N
leatsa    le        P
foclóir   foclóir   N
Ioruaise  Ioruais   N
a         a         T
sheoladh  seol      V
chúm      chuig     P
```

INTER-BI 246 tokens (26% of the English tokens) represent code-switching for the purposes of providing comprehension for two groups of followers (Irish speakers and non-Irish speakers)

```
Lón       lón       N
sa        i         P
Spéir     spéir     N
/         /         ,
MEN       MEN       EN    INTER-BI
AT        AT        EN    INTER-BI
LUNCH     LUNCH     EN    INTER-BI
FILM      FILM      EN    INTER-BI
```

WORD Interestingly, our data only contains two instances of word level code-switching. This ran counter to our intuition before examining the corpus data, as examples of this kind are heard in the spoken language quite frequently. The two tagged examples both use the Irish emphatic prefix 'an-' with an English root: *an-talent* 'a lot of talent'; *an-time* 'a great time'. It is possible, of course, to find other examples of this word level switching on Twitter by focused searching (e.g. examples of verbs with the gerund suffix '-áil': *creepáil, buzzáil, textáil, snapchatáil, flirtáil*, etc.). However, our data suggest that the relative frequency of such types may not be as high as our intuition leads us to believe.

```
tá           bí        V
an-talent    talent    EN    WORD
go           go        P
deo          deo       N
```

```
agaibh      ag      P
in          i       P
Éirinn      Éire    ^
```

INTRA(+EN-POS) 297 tokens (31% of the English tokens) are used in an intra-sentential manner, that is to say that these English tokens are inserted comfortably within the syntax of Irish phrases. Figure 1 shows the distribution of the EN POS tags for intra-sentential code-switching. This feature is of the most interest to us, and is therefore described in more detail in the next section.

```
Don't     Don't     EN  INTRA-V
forget    forget    EN  INTRA-V
to        to        EN  INTRA-P
use       use       EN  INTRA-V
the       the       EN  INTRA-D
cúpla     cúpla     D
focal     focal     N
ag        ag        P
obair     obair     N
agus      agus      &
ar        ar        P
scoil     scoil     N
```

INTRA+POS	POS meaning
INTRA-N	Noun
INTRA-V	Verb
INTRA-A	Adjective
INTRA-P	Preposition
INTRA-D	Determiner
INTRA-R	Adverb
INTRA-!	Interjection
INTRA-O	Pronoun
INTRA-G	General
INTRA-&	Conjunction
INTRA-VN	Verbal Noun
INTRA-T	Particle

Table 1: Explanation of fine-grained (INTRA+) intra-sentential tags

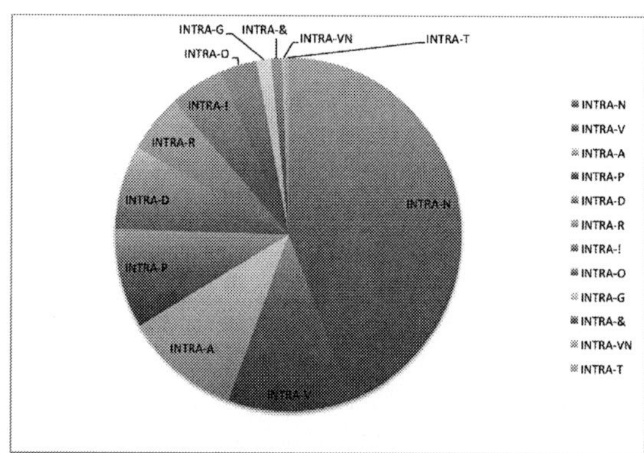

Figure 1: Distribution of INTRA tags, showing the syntactic role of code-switched tokens. Tag descriptions are given in Table 1

4.2 Nature of INTRA code-switching in Irish tweets

One striking outcome of preliminary observations of this work is the distribution of syntactic patterns that arise within intra-sentential code-switching between Irish and English. There is a clear ease with which English nouns are used to replace Irish nouns in a single instance. For example *Figiúirí nua tally do Chonamara* 'New tally fig-

ures for Connemara'. In this instance, the English word 'tally' is part of a noun compound.[6] In Irish, the head of noun compound is the first noun (`figiúirí` tally) – in English it is the last (tally `figures`). In addition, the position of the adjective *nua* 'new' follows the rules of Irish syntax by following rather than preceding the head noun. Several similar noun-adjective examples exist in the corpus: *keyboards `beag`* 'small keyboards', *podcast úr* 'new podcast', *an album nua* 'the new album', *an stuff corcra* 'the purple stuff'. It is interesting to note that in these final two cases, there exist Gaelicized spellings of the code-switched words, *albam* and *stuif* respectively. In the first case at least, had the Irish form been intended, one would have *an t-albam nua* to satisfy Irish grammatical constraints related to the gender of the noun.

The relative infrequency of intra-sentential verb usage is particularly interesting when we consider the variations across English and Irish with respect to word order (SVO vs VSO). We observe that 5 out of the 34 INTRA-V (English verb) occurrences occur alone in an Irish context. (e.g. *Wish nach raibh aon obair le déanamh agam* 'Wish I didn't have work to do') All other 29 instances are part of an Irish string of two or more tokens (e.g. *am éigin an bhliain seo sounds good* 'some time this year sounds good'). Interestingly, Müller (1999) observed a similarly rare switching of verbs from Irish to Latin in historical texts.

---

[6]Interestingly, the Gaelicized spelling *teailí* is recorded in dictionaries and is seen occasionally in Irish writing.

4.3 Automatic POS tagging and detection of code-switching

We also reproduced the automatic POS tagging experiments from Lynn et al. (2015) with the addition of the EN tag in order to evaluate the impact of the slightly richer tagset on tagger performance, and to assess this as an approach to detecting code-switched segments. Due to the relative infrequency of code-switching types (INTRA, INTER, INTER-BI, WORD), we do not yet have enough data to train an effective tagger for this level of annotation, so the results below involve only the introduction of the tag EN.

In Table 2, the results given for the models Base-Morf and NormMorf (using the Morfette tagger of Chrupala et al. (2008)) and ArkLemma#URL@ (using the ARK tagger of Gimpel et al. (2011)) are the same as those of Lynn et al. (2015), to which we refer the reader for full experimental details. The results given with the suffix +EN repeat the same experiments but this time based on the training and test data that we have retagged, using the EN tag for code-switched tokens. Given the relative infrequency of the EN tag in the overall corpus, it is not surprising that the results change only slightly. The slight improvements coming from the introduction of the EN tag might be explained in part by the use of the G tag as a kind of "catch-all", making it difficult for the tagger to learn generalizations over examples of G tags. For example, in the original training corpus without the EN tag, there many sequences of two or more consecutive G tags. As a consequence, the taggers of Lynn et al. (2015) sometimes incorrectly assign G tags to one or more Irish words following an English word, but this seems to happen less often after introduction of the separate EN tag.

5 Inter-annotator Agreement

In order to assess consistency, levels of bias, and reliability of the annotated data, we carried out an Inter-Annotator Agreement (IAA) study. There are a number of metrics used widely to calculate IAA in classification tasks (Artstein and Poesio, 2008). In this study, we report IAA between two annotators using Cohen's Kappa (Cohen, 1960):

$$\kappa = \frac{P(A) - P(E)}{1 - P(E)}$$

where $P(A)$ is the proportion of observed agreement among annotators, and $P(E)$ is the propor-

Training Data	Dev	Test
Baseline		
Rule-Based Tagger	85.07	83.51
Morfette		
BaseMorf	86.77	88.67
BaseMorf+EN	87.16	88.64
NormMorf	87.94	88.74
NormMorf+EN	**88.06**	**89.22**
ARK		
ArkLemma#URL@	**91.46**	91.89
ArkLemma#URL@+EN	91.23	**91.98**

Table 2: Changes in POS-tagging accuracy following separate labelling of English tokens (+EN indicates new experiments).

tion of expected agreement. By correcting for $P(E)$, this measurement accounts for the fact that the annotators are expected to agree a proportion of times just by chance. Di Eugenio and Glass (2004) present the calculation of Cohen's $P(E)$ as:

$$P(E) = \sum_{j} p_{j,1} \times p_{j,2}$$

where $p_{j,a}$ is the overall proportion of items assigned to a label j by annotator a.

For this study, we presented all 1496 tweets to the annotators. Annotators first received instructions to annotate all English tokens as 'EN'. For each English token, according to the code-switching categories described in Section 2.1, a new tag was to be inserted in the next column (INTER, INTER-BI, INTRA or WORD). We refer to these as *coarse-grained tags*. For each INTRA tag we also asked the annotators to identify the POS-tag for the English token (e.g INTRA-N (noun), INTRA-V (verb), etc). We refer to these as *fine-grained tags*. 943 tokens in the corpus are English tokens, and as such our kappa score is based on the agreement of the labelling of these tokens.

We achieved a kappa agreement rate of 0.69 on coarse-grained tags and 0.74 on fine-grained tags. On closer inspection, there were a couple of clear explanations for the coarse-grained tagging disagreements. Some cases involved confusion between INTER vs INTER-BI, and INTER vs INTRA. As an instance of INTER usually consists of a string of tokens (e.g. 'a rock and a hard place'), a single misinterpretation can lead to multiple instances of tag disagreement.

We use Landis and Koch (1977)'s metric shown in Table 3 for interpretation of our Kappa results.

Kappa value	Strength of Agreement
< 0.00	None
0.00 − 0.20	Slight
0.21 − 0.40	Fair
0.41 − 0.60	Moderate
0.61 − 0.80	Substantial
0.81 − 1.00	Almost Perfect

Table 3: Landis and Koch's interpretation of Cohens's Kappa

While our results are regarded as substantial agreement we will take this as an opportunity to identify the areas of confusion and to revise our annotation guidelines for future labelling work.

6 Conclusion and Future Directions

We have reported on the enhancement of a corpus of POS-tagged Irish tweets with code-switching annotations and provided a categorisation of code-switching types of Irish UGC. We have also provided a quantitative report with respect to the distribution of code-switched tweets and tag types in the corpus.[7]

We have also reported more accurate automatic POS tagging results for these tweets, based on the inclusion of updated EN labels.

Our study has revealed that Irish speaking online users switch effortlessly and effectively between Irish and English. This ease demonstrates the clever mix across the syntax paradigms of both languages and supports the argument that code-switching is indeed a reflection of advanced grammatical ability. The various different types of code-switching employed suggested different motivations for this linguistic behaviour.

In terms of future work, the natural progression for this study would be to increase the size of the dataset so that more instances of code-switching can be observed and analysed. Of course, after having observed the disagreements amongst annotators in our IAA study, we will need to update the annotation guideline to make the instructions much clearer and to avoid ambiguity.

In future work, we would also like to take a more socio-linguistic approach to our analysis. We would like to investigate users' motivation for code-switching and assess whether linguistic patterns provide clues as to why and when English

text is inserted into Irish tweets. For example, in some instances, we observe that English noun phrases are used where there is no official Irish term for a concept, and in other instances where there is an official Irish term that may not be known to the speaker (or if known, not preferred). This type of information would be a useful source of data for language planning and terminology development.

Given that Stam (2017) notes that "it appears that code-switching in medieval Irish texts may be both a functional communicative device used to structure a text and an unconscious expression of bilingual identity for a like-minded audience", we believe our corpus will provide an interesting dataset to help identify whether this holds true today.

One likely future application of this corpus is to build a tool to automatically identify code-switching in Irish online content. Despite it being a challenging task, there has been much progress in this area, with notable impact on a number of downstream applications, as outlined by Çetinoğlu et al. (2016). Yet, we note that our own data set is still not large enough to support state-of-the-art data-driven approaches. Further development of this corpus is therefore required.

In addition, we see this data set as a starting point for a treebank of Irish user-generated content. Parsing code-switched text is an area of research attracting much attention, and for this reason we have labelled the POS-tag of the switched tokens. Again, this is simply a starting point and much larger data set will be required before a data-driven system can be developed.

7 Acknowledgements

The first author's work is funded by the Irish Government Department of Culture, Heritage and the Gaeltacht under the GaelTech Project, and is also supported by Science Foundation Ireland in the ADAPT Centre (Grant 13/RC/2106) at Dublin City University.

8 Bibliographical References

References

Afli, Haithem, Sorcha McGuire, and Andy Way. 2017. Sentiment translation for low-resourced languages: Experiments on Irish General Election tweets. In *Proceedings of the 8th International Conference on Intelligent Text Processing and Computational Linguistics*, Budapest, Hungary.

---

[7]Available to download from `https://github.com/tlynn747/IrishTwitterPOS/tree/master/Data/morfette-CS`

Artstein, Ron and Massimo Poesio. 2008. Inter-coder agreement for computational linguistics. *Computational Linguistics*, 34(4):555–596, December.

Atkinson, David and Helen Kelly-Holmes. 2011. Codeswitching, identity and ownership in Irish radio comedy. *Journal of Pragmatics*, 43(1):251 – 260.

Bannett Kastor, Tina. 2008. Code-mixing in biliterate and multiliterate Irish literary texts. *Asociación Española de Estudios Irlandeses (AEDEI)*, 3:29–41.

Caulfield, John. 2013. *A social network analysis of Irish language use in social media*. Ph.D. thesis, Cardiff University.

Çetinoğlu, Özlem, Sarah Schulz, and Ngoc Thang Vu. 2016. Challenges of computational processing of code-switching. In *Proceedings of the Second Workshop on Computational Approaches to Code Switching*, pages 1–11, Austin, Texas, November. Association for Computational Linguistics.

Chrupala, Grzegorz, Georgiana Dinu, and Josef van Genabith. 2008. Learning morphology with Morfette. In *Proceedings of the International Conference on Language Resources and Evaluation, LREC 2008, 26 May - 1 June 2008, Marrakech, Morocco*.

Cohen, J. 1960. A Coefficient of Agreement for Nominal Scales. *Educational and Psychological Measurement*, 20(1):37.

Di Eugenio, Barbara and Michael Glass. 2004. The Kappa statistic: a second look. *Computational Linguistics*, 30(1):95–101, March.

Dowling, Meghan, Teresa Lynn, and Andy Way. 2017. A crowd-sourcing approach for translations of minority language user-generated content (UGC). In *Proceedings of The First Workshop on Social Media and User Generated Content Machine Translation*, Prague, Czech Republic.

Dumville, David. 1990. Latin and Irish in the Annals of ulster, a.d. 431- 1050. *Histories and Pseudo-Histories of the Insular Middle Ages*, pages 320–341.

Espinosa, Aurelio, 1917. *The Pacific Ocean in History*, chapter Speech Mixture in New Mexico: the influence of English language on New Mexican Spanish. New York MacMillan.

Gimpel, Kevin, Nathan Schneider, Brendan O'Connor, Dipanjan Das, Daniel Mills, Jacob Eisenstein, Michael Heilman, Dani Yogatama, Jeffrey Flanigan, and Noah A. Smith. 2011. Part-of-speech tagging for Twitter: Annotation, features, and experiments. In *Proceedings of the 49th Annual Meeting of the Association for Computational Linguistics: Human Language Technologies: Short Papers - Volume 2*, HLT '11, pages 42–47, Stroudsburg, PA, USA. Association for Computational Linguistics.

Grosjean, François. 2010. *Bilingual: Life and Reality*. Harvard University Press.

Hickey, Tina. 2009. Code-switching and borrowing in Irish. *Journal of Sociolinguistics*, 13(5):670–688.

Joshi, Aravind K. 1982. Processing of sentences with intra-sentential code-switching. In *Proceedings of the 9th International Conference on Computational Linguistics, COLING '82, Prague, Czechoslovakia, July 5-10, 1982*, pages 145–150.

Lackaff, Derek and William J. Moner. 2016. Local languages, global networks: Mobile design for minority language users. In *Proceedings of the 34th ACM International Conference on the Design of Communication*, SIGDOC '16, pages 14:1–14:9, New York, NY, USA. ACM.

Landis, J. Richard and Gary G. Koch. 1977. The measurement of observer agreement for categorical data. In *Biometrics*, volume 33, pages 159–174. International Biometric Society.

Ní Laoire, Siobhán, 2016. *Irish-English Code-switching: A Sociolinguistic Perspective*, pages 81–106. Palgrave Macmillan UK, London.

Lynn, Teresa, Kevin Scannell, and Eimear Maguire. 2015. Minority Language Twitter. Part-of-Speech Tagging and Analysis of Irish Tweets. In *Proceedings of the 1st Workshop on Noisy User-generated Text (W-NUT 2015)*, Beijing, China.

Minocha, Akshay and Francis M. Tyers. 2014. Subsegmental language detection in Celtic language text. In *Proceedings of the Celtic Language Technology Workshop (CLTW), co-located with COLING 2014*.

Molina, Giovanni, Nicolas Rey-Villamizar, Thamar Solorio, Fahad AlGhamdi, Mahmoud Ghoneim, Abdelati Hawwari, and Mona Diab. 2016. Overview for the Second shared task on language identification in code-switched data. EMNLP 2016.

Muysken, Pieter. 1995. *One speaker, two languages: Cross-disciplinary perspectives on code-switching*. Cambridge University Press, Cambridge, England.

Müller, Nicole. 1999. Kodewechsel in der irischen Übersetzungsliteratur: exempla et desiderata. *Übersetzung, Adaptation und Akkulturation im insularen Mittelalter*, pages 73–86.

Nguyen, Dong, A. Seza Doğruöz, Carolyn P. Rosé, and Franciska de Jong. 2016. Computational Sociolinguistics: A Survey. *Comput. Linguist.*, 42(3):537–593, September.

Rosner, Mike and Paulseph-John Farrugia. 2007. A tagging algorithm for mixed language identification in a noisy domain. In *INTERSPEECH*, pages 190–193. ISCA.

Solorio, Thamar and Yang Liu. 2008. Part-of-speech tagging for English-Spanish code-switched text. In *Proceedings of the Conference on Empirical Methods in Natural Language Processing*, EMNLP '08, pages 1051–1060, Stroudsburg, PA, USA. Association for Computational Linguistics.

Solorio, Thamar, Elizabeth Blair, Suraj Maharjan, Steven Bethard, Mona Diab, Mahmoud Gohneim, Abdelati Hawwari, Fahad AlGhamdi, Julia Hirschberg, Alison Chang, and Pascale Fung. 2014. Overview for the First shared task on language identification in code-switched data. In *Proceedings of The First Workshop on Computational Approaches to Code Switching, held in conjunction with EMNLP 2014.*, pages 62–72, Doha, Qatar. ACL.

Stam, Nike. 2017. *A typology of code-switching in the Commentary to the Félire Óengusso.* Ph.D. thesis, Utrecht University.

Stenson, Nancy. 1993. English influence on Irish: The last 100 years. *Journal of Celtic linguistics*, 2:107–128.

Embedding English to Welsh MT in a Private Company

Myfyr Prys
Cymen Cyf
Bangor University
Myfyr@Cymen.co.uk

Dewi Bryn Jones
Bangor University
d.b.jones@bangor.ac.uk

Abstract

This paper reports on a Knowledge Transfer Partnership (KTP) project that aimed to implement machine translation technology at a Welsh Language Service Provider, Cymen Cyf[1]. The project involved leveraging the company's large supply of previous translations in order to train custom domain-specific translation engines for its various clients. BLEU scores achieved ranged from 59.06 for the largest domain-specific engine to 48.53 to the smallest. A small experiment using the TAUS DQF productivity evaluation tool (Görög, 2014) was also run on the highest-scoring translation engine, which showed an average productivity gain of 30% across all translators. Domain-specific engines were ultimately successfully introduced into the workflow for two main clients, although a lack of domain specific data proved problematic for others. Various techniques such as domain-adaptation as well as improved tagging of previous translations may ameliorate this situation in the future.

1 Introduction

The translation industry in Wales has seen substantial growth over the past few decades, particularly in response to political pressures. Government legislation currently obliges all public sector bodies to produce bilingual versions of all public-facing documents, while sociocultural pressure has also influenced private businesses to invest in translation services. But the mounting demand for translation services presents challenges as well as opportunities for Welsh Linguistic Service Providers (hereafter LSPs). LSPs need to balance expenditure (on staff and equipment) with the capacity to deal with existing demands for services. Technology provides one answer to this challenge, as the work of a single translator can be extended.

A report by Bangor University's Language Technology Unit (Prys et al., 2009) found that using various kinds of translation technology could raise the economic productivity of the Welsh translation industry by 40% and could also prevent the undercutting of translation services by foreign providers leveraging new technology (2009: 23). The uptake of translation technology in Wales has been slow however, with various surveys (Prys et al., 2009 and Andrews 2010) reporting percentages of Welsh translators using translation environment technology as low as 49% and 50%, compared to the figures of 82% (Lagoudaki, 2006) and 65% (EU Commission, 2017) reported at the international level[2] and in the UK respectively. While low adoption rates for new technology may seem inevitable in the context of a lesser-resourced language, the Welsh Government has made the expansion of such tools an important part of its strategy to reach a million Welsh speakers by 2050 (Welsh Government, 2019: 34).

© 2019 The authors. This article is licensed under a Creative Commons 4.0 licence, no derivative works, attribution, CC-BY-ND.

[1] Cymen Cyf have given their permission to be discussed as part of this study.

[2] The survey was completed by 874 respondents from 54 countries. The author does not provide information on the linguistic backgrounds of respondents, but does mention that the survey had to be completed in English, which could mean that results were biased towards "English-speaking professionals" (Lagoudaki, 2006: 6).

One tool which the Welsh Government has to promote specialist training and skills in the private sector is the Knowledge Transfer Partnership, or KTP. KTPs involve a partnership in which a university works together with a private business in order to transfer academic knowledge relating to a specific field. The project described in this paper involved a KTP between a Welsh University and a North Wales LSP, Cymen Cyf.

2 Cymen as an innovative Welsh LSP

Cymen was first established during the mid-eighties amid a wave of expansion in demand for English to Welsh translation (Andrews, 2015). The demographic profile of staff at Cymen fits the data reported by Prys et al. (2009), with a workforce which is primarily rural, female and educated to an advanced level. Staff are almost all recipients of further degrees in Welsh, which provides the fundamental skillset for the challenging task of English to Welsh translation. Cymen belies the typical image of a Welsh translation company, however, in that it has embraced a technological approach to translation. The use of translation memories[3] and termbases is well-established at the company, partly as a result of a KTP project in 2000 which led to the adoption of SDL's Translator's Workbench software, and later Trados SDL.

An analysis of Cymen's translation memories shows that at least 300,000 words are translated by the company's 16 translators each month using the Trados translation environment. Machine translation had not been implemented in the company until the advent of this project. Translation companies generally have two main options in this regard: to use a pre-existing paid service or to integrate some technical expertise into the company in order to implement an open source solution.

The first option is problematic for a variety of reasons: companies can quickly be locked in to services with little flexibility or control, and consequently may not be able to make the most of their translation engines. The second option, which involves integrating technical expertise into the company, has the advantage of leveraging free, open-source software with a flexible implementation. In practice this means that a company can create custom translation engines using their own data, while avoiding any potential data-protection concerns which may arise from having to hand over data to a multinational company. The aim of the KTP project was to realize the second option, using Cymen's existing archive of past translations to train domain-specific translation engines. Where possible, we also hoped to transfer the relevant expertise to the company's own staff.

3 Related work on MT

Previous attempts to create machine translation systems for the Welsh-English language pair are reported in Jones and Eisle (2006) and Tyers and Donnelly (2009). Jones and Eisle developed a baseline statistical machine translation system using Pharaoh (Koehn, 2004), a precursor to Moses SMT. They trained Welsh to English and English to Welsh engines on a 510,813 segment corpus extracted from the Record of Proceedings of the National Assembly for Wales. The authors report a BLEU[4] score of 40.22 for the Welsh to English engine and 36.17 for the English to Welsh engine.

Tyers and Donnelly (2009) developed a Welsh to English module for the rule-based machine translation (RBMT) system *Apertium*. The BLEU scores they report are relatively low as one might expect for an RBMT system, with a score of 15.68 for the Record of Proceedings of the National Assembly corpus. The authors argue, however, that such systems are crucial for lesser resourced languages like Welsh, drawing attention to the lack of publically available training corpora with open licensing. Beyond open source implementations, private companies such as Google and Microsoft provide English-Welsh translation engines that can be used within

---

[3] Translation memories are databases that store previous translations as segmented text. These segments can be retrieved and re-used to substantially speed-up repetitive translation work.

[4] BLEU (Papineni et al., 2001) is an algorithm that enables the automatic evaluation of a translation engine's output on a scale of 0 to 100, with higher scores indicating better translations. It works through comparing the engine's output with a reference translation of the same text, which is produced by a human translator.

translation software. A recent study by Screen (2018) offers evidence that using Google Translate within Trados for English to Welsh post-editing tripled translators' productivity, and cut typing by half. Although clearly effective, these services have some drawbacks including the need for payment and a lack of flexibility.

In terms of related language pairs, the ADAPT Centre team at Dublin City University have reported on their English to Irish Moses SMT engine *Tapadóir*, which was developed for use at a Government department responsible for Irish language affairs (Dowling et al., 2015). The team achieved an optimal BLEU score by combining in- and out of domain data, drawing on a mixture of publically available corpora, web-crawled data and domain-specific translation memory data. However, the relative sparsity of the available data and the comparative complexity of Irish morphology reportedly caused some problems. The team later developed an automatic post-editing module (APE) that allowed correction of certain repeated errors caused by these sparse data issues (Dowling et al., 2016). Dowling et al. (2018) reports on a comparison between the hybrid Moses SMT *Tapadóir* implementation and a newly developed NMT engine trained on the same data set. *Tapadóir* outperformed the baseline NMT engine by 8.75 BLEU points, although using byte pair encoding (Sennrich, 2016) with the NMT engine narrowed the gap slightly to 6.4 BLEU points. The authors argue that the poor performance of NMT in this case is largely due to the Irish language target exhibiting "many of the known challenges that NMT currently struggles with (data scarcity, long sentences and rich morphology)" (2018: 18).

Attempts to implement NMT for translation into another under-resourced and morphologically complex language, Basque, achieved more positive results in a recent study (Etchegoyhen et al., 2018) which found that an NMT system outperformed SMT by 4 BLEU points in Spanish to Basque machine translation. The best explanation for this discrepancy lies in the relative sizes of the corpora used for training. *Tapadóir* was trained on 108,796 parallel segments, while the MODELA engine was trained on 3,345,763 — a vast difference. Given that NMT is known to suffer from data scarcity, it seems clear that the greatest challenge facing lesser-resourced languages is the requisition of sufficient data suitable for training.

4 Data collection and preparation

The MT system implemented is based on the Welsh National Language Technologies Portal's (Prys and Jones, 2018) provision of Moses SMT (Jones et al., 2016).[5] This is a baseline implementation of Moses SMT with a simplified interface and the ability to run a Moses server instance from a Docker container image. Some advantages of the implementation are that it simplifies installation as well as subsequent training, tokenization and truecasing processes, streamlines the use of a Moses server API in third-party applications, and provides Docker containerization options. The machine translation provision was further expanded during the KTP project to include automatic tuning and evaluation of the Moses model using MERT[6] (Och, 2003) and BLEU (Papineni et al., 2002) respectively. Translation engines are trained using TMX files (an xml specification for transferring translation data between different localization software) extracted from Cymen's various translation memories.

TMXs were chosen as our main focus because they contain source and target segments already aligned, dispensing with the need for complicated alignment processes, and normally contain relatively clean data which has been carefully curated by the company. They were also convenient because the company's archive of previous translations was already largely available in this format.

Cymen's translation memory workflow revolves around a policy of assigning a TM to each regular client (although they also have some general domain memories, such as 'health' or 'education'). For instance, in the case of a fictional client named *Ideore*, the process would work as follows:

---

1.   Work from the client becomes frequent, so the company creates a dedicated *Ideore* translation memory and termbase.

2.   These resources are consolidated into a project template file that facilitates the creation of *Ideore* projects by admin staff.

3.   *Ideore* projects are allocated to specific translators based on availability and expertise, and the translation memory starts to fill.

In order to process a TMX file for training translation engines, certain pre-processing steps are necessary. Welsh and English segments are extracted from the TMX files and are stored in an SQL database, having been tagged for metadata such as domain (usually the client's name), language pair, date, and more. Different permutations of data can then be selected and exported to parallel text files for training and testing. Following this the data is randomized and split into three parts. Two held-out data sets are created - a 3,000 segment test set for evaluation with BLEU and a 2,000 segment tuning set for tuning with MERT. The language model is created from the target side of the training corpus. Finally, segments from both the training set and tuning set are removed from the main training corpus and language model to avoid skewing the evaluation and tuning steps.

5   Training the engines

We decided to set an arbitrary threshold of a million Welsh words before attempting to evaluate the baseline capability of engines trained on such data. Figure 1 below shows all of Cymen's TMs arranged by number of Welsh words.

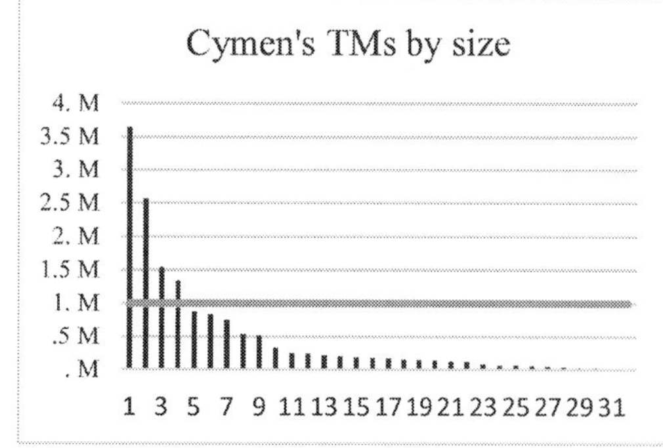

Figure 1. Each of Cymen's TMs arranged by number of Welsh words, from largest to smallest

As can be seen in the chart, only 4 of our TMs are currently large enough to satisfy this criterion.

Table 1 displays BLEU scores for engines trained from these TMs client-specific TMX files, as well as the general-domain Cymen translation engine. As might be expected based on previous research (e.g. Koehn 2001), the scores seem to be related to the size of the corpus used for training as well as the specificity of the domain. The highest scoring engine is the domain-specific engine 1, which was trained on a 174,354 segment parallel corpus of data relating to a client in a technology-related domain. Although the size of the parallel corpus used for training is an obvious contributor to its relatively high score, the nature of the domain, which consists of a highly technical and repetitive register, also seems to be a factor.

Translation Engine ID	Number of Welsh words	Number of segments	BLEU score
1	3.65 million	174,354	59.06
2	2.56 million	130,235	58.75
3	1.54 million	83,745	50.92
4	1.34 million	74,840	48.53
Cymen	65.3 million	3,985,674	54.23

Table 1. BLEU scores and corpus size for the five top translation engines

Engines three and four had substantially lower scores, reflecting the smaller corpora used for training. For comparison, we also trained a general domain corpus consisting of all of Cymen's combined data (named Cymen in table 1). Although trained on a comparatively large data set, translation engines 1 and 2 still outperform this engine in terms of BLEU score, which provides some indication of the value of using domain-specific engines.

6   Engine effectiveness

To gain a general idea of the effectiveness of our engines, we used the TAUS DQF evaluation tool (Görög, 2014) to carry out a productivity test on segments automatically translated by our highest-scoring domain-specific translation engine (ID 1, BLEU score 59.06 – see table 1 above). Eight translators were selected to translate 50 in-domain segments from a held-out data set, with a total of

905 words. The segments were randomly selected before being submitted to the TAUS DQF evaluation tool. TAUS DQF automatically shuffles the segments and presents half to be translated from scratch (i.e. without the machine-translated output) and half to be post-edited (with the machine-translated output). The tool then times the completion of each segment and generates a report based on the average completion time for both conditions.

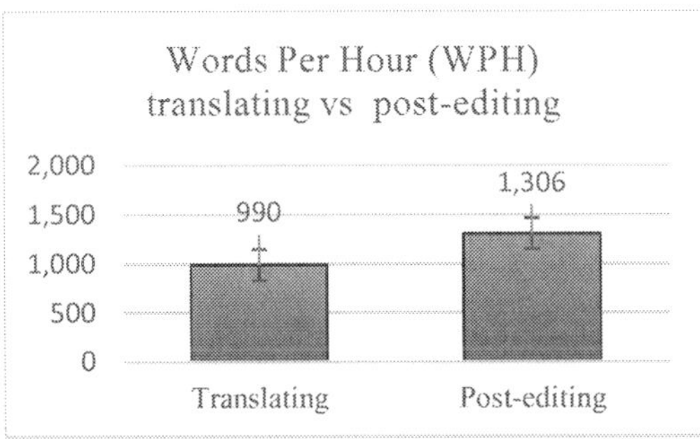

Figure 3. The average WPH of Cymen's translators while translating vs post-editing

The results (figure 3) show that the participants produced 1,372 words per hour on average while post-editing as opposed to 1,055 words per hour while translating from scratch. Individual results for the translators (figure 4) show quite considerable variation, although all translators performed more quickly in the post-editing condition.

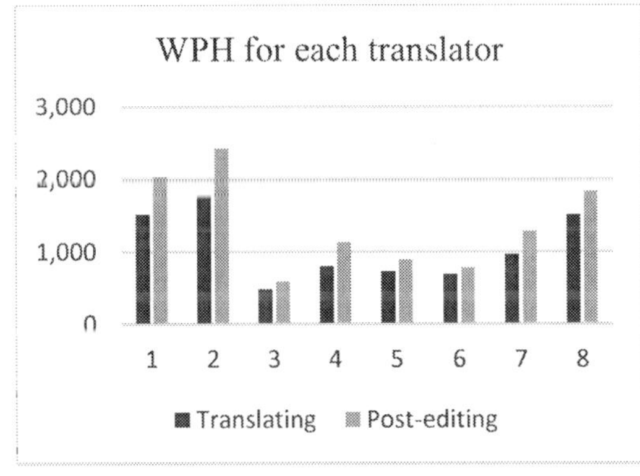

Figure 4. WPH per condition for each translator

The result of this analysis suggests that using a machine of this quality can increase productivity across all translators by 30%, while individual gains vary from a high of 41% to a low of 14%.

7 Implementing the engines

Once we were satisfied that the quality of the engines was of a satisfactory level, the engines needed to be embedded in the company's translation environment software. An app for integrating the engines was designed on the basis of an open-source C# solution available on GitHub[7]. In order to allow the selection of multiple engines, distinct engines are run from their own Docker containers, which can each then be selected from within the Trados interface.

Before the engines could be fully integrated into translators' workflows, the company's management team trialed their performance personally for a probationary period. Based on this the management decided to start using engines 1 and 2 in every project for the relevant clients. As engines 3 and 4 were not considered of a high enough quality to use routinely, we decided not to implement them for the time being. Given that there is a clear link between the size of a domain-specific engine and its effectiveness, and that the company's store of data for each client is always growing, it was decided that we would attempt to retrain using these client's data at a later date. It was also decided that we would start gathering analytic data on the size and relative growth of translation memories on a monthly basis. This should allow the company to make informed decisions concerning whether data belonging to a particular client has reached a point where training an effective translation engine for it has become viable.

8 Reception by translators

In order to take possible resistance from translators to machine translation into account, we introduced the engines into their workflow gradually. Firstly, we waited until the output of the translation engines was of a relatively high quality - based on the management team's assessment - before introducing them into the daily workflows. This hopefully mitigated the prospect of poor machine translation irreparably damaging translators' feelings towards the technology. The practical implementation of the engines was also

---

[7]https://github.com/OpenNMT/Plugins/tree/master/SDL%20Trados%20Plugin

relatively subtle, with engine allocation happening at management level, meaning that translators did not need to take any actions themselves. Finally, a series of four workshops were held for all staff, where the KTP assistant was able to describe the basic principles of the technology. Particular emphasis was placed on the fact that machine translation is a post-editing tool, which cannot replace human translators. It was also stressed that productivity gains associated with less typing and additional time can make the translator's work less laborious and more comfortable.

In general the company's reception of the technology has been positive. The most obvious manifestation of this is that engines 1 and 2 are now used routinely for translating those clients' respective domain-specific data, which taken together represent a large proportion of the company's daily output. The general domain *Cymen* engine is also now used frequently for translating data for smaller clients that have data particularly suitable for machine translation. One feature that was repeatedly praised by the translators was the autosuggest capability[8], which prompts the user with suggested words or phrases extracted from the translation engine as they type. This was seen as particularly useful because translators were able to leverage useful elements of an engine's output even when the segment as a whole was not perfect.

9   Future research

Following the successful implementation of machine translation during the KTP, both partners are interested in extending the capabilities of the translation system. Obvious candidates for such improvements include neural and/or hybrid translation systems, which have not yet been reported in open source implementations for Welsh. However, the primary challenge facing Cymen is the lack of sufficient data for training domain-specific engines for the majority of its clients. Exploring domain adaptation techniques (e.g. Axelrod et al., 2011), which allow out-of-domain data to be leveraged for domain-specific engines, offers one way of dealing with the scarcity of data for some domains discussed above. Otherwise, the main way that Cymen can improve its translation engines is through the

natural growth of its translation memory archive through daily translation work, which continues apace.

10   Conclusion

This paper has discussed the implementation of open-source machine translation software at a Welsh translation company. We have shown that leveraging a private company's archive of previous translations to train domain-specific translation engines is a relatively straightforward task, although the success of the endeavour is to some extent dependent on the company storing translations with some kind of metadata indicating domain. This shows the importance of educating the translation sector in Wales (and beyond) in the value of such data and the importance of storing in such a way that its usefulness for future MT tasks is maximized.

References

Andrews, T. (2015) Cyd-destun gwleidyddol a chymdeithasol cyfieithu yn y Gymru gyfoes. In: Prys, D & Trefor, R. (Eds). *Ysgrifau a Chanllawiau Cyfieithu*. [Online]. Carmarthen: Coleg Cymraeg Cenedlaethol. Available at: https://llyfrgell.porth.ac.uk/media/ysgrifau-a-chanllawiau-cyfieithu-delyth-prys-arobat-trefor-goln [Retrieved: 27/01/2016].

Dowling, M., Cassidy, L., Maguire, E., Lynn, T., Srivastava, A., and Judge, J. (2015). Tapadóir: Developing a statistical machine translation engine and associated resources for Irish. In *Proceedings of the The Fourth LRL Workshop: "Language Technologies in support of Less-Resourced Languages"*, Poznan, Poland.

Dowling, M., Lynn, T., Graham, Y., and Judge, J. (2016). English to Irish machine translation with automatic post-editing. In *2nd Celtic Language Technology Workshop* (pp. 42-54), Paris, France.

Dowling, M., Lynn, T., Poncelas, A., & Way, A. (2018). SMT versus NMT: Preliminary Comparisons for Irish. In *Workshop on Technologies for MT of Low Resource Languages* (p.p. 12-20), Boston, USA.

European Commission Representation in the UK, Chartered Institute of Linguists and the Institute of Translation and Interpreting. (2017) *2016 UK Translator Survey - Final Report*. Available online at: https://ec.europa.eu/unitedkingdom/sites/unit

---

[8] This feature is part of Trados software

edkingdom/files/ukts2016-final-report-web_-_18_may_2017.pdf Retrieved: [28/06/2019]. Cymraeg 2050:

Görög, A. (2014). Quantifying and benchmarking quality: the TAUS Dynamic Quality Framework. *Tradumàtica*, (12), 443-454.

Jones, D.and Andreas E. (2006). Phrase-based statistical machine translation between English and Welsh. In *Strategies for developing machine translation for minority languages (5th SALT-MIL workshop on Minority Languages)*, LREC-2006 (p.p. 75-78), Genoa, Italy.

Jones, D.B., Prys, D., Ghazzali, S. and Robertson, P. (2016) Facilitating the Multilingual Single Digital Market: Case Studies in Software Containerization of Language Technologies. In *Proceedings of META-FORUM 2016*, Lisbon, Portugal.

Lagoudaki, E. (2006). Translation memories survey 2006: Users' perceptions around TM use. In *proceedings of the ASLIB International Conference Translating & the Computer* (Vol. 28, No. 1, pp. 1-29). London, UK.

Och, F. J. (2003). Minimum error rate training in statistical machine translation. In *Proceedings of the 41st Annual Meeting on Association for Computational Linguistics-Volume 1* (pp. 160-167). Sapporo, Japan.

Papineni, K., Roukos, S., Ward, T., & Zhu, W. J. (2002). BLEU: a method for automatic evaluation of machine translation. In *Proceedings of the 40th annual meeting on association for computational linguistics* (pp. 311-318). Philadelphia, USA.

Prys, D. & Jones, D.B. (2018) *National Language Technologies Portals for LRLs: a Case Study*. In: Vetulani Z., Mariani J., Kubis M. (eds) Lecture Notes in Artificial Intelligence. Springer.

Prys, D. et al. (2009). Gwell Offer Technoleg Cyfieithu ar gyfer y Diwydiant Cyfieithu yng Nghymru: Arolwg Dadansoddol [Online]. Bangor: Language Technologies Unit, Canolfan Bedwyr Available at: https://goo.gl/52ZYfj [Retrieved: 01/05/2019].

Screen, B. (2018). Defnyddio Cyfieithu Awtomatig a Chof Cyfieithu wrth gyfieithu o'r Saesneg i'r Gymraeg: Astudiaeth ystadegol o ymdrech, cynhyrchedd ac ansawdd gan ddefnyddio data Cofnodwyr Trawiadau Bysell a Thracio Llygaid. (Unpublished PhD Thesis). Cardiff University, Wales. Available online at: http://orca.cf.ac.uk/111362/

Sennrich, R., Haddow, B., & Birch, A. (2015). Neural machine translation of rare words with subword units. *arXiv preprint arXiv:1508.07909*.

Thierry Etchegoyhen, Eva Martínez, Andoni Azpeitia, Gorka Labaka, Iñaki Alegria, Itziar Cortes, Amaia Jauregi, Igor Ellakuria, Maite Martin eta Eusebi Calonge (2018) Neural Machine Translation of Basque EAMT 2018. Alicante.

Tyers, F., & Donnelly, K. (2009). apertium-cy - a collaboratively-developed free RBMT system for Welsh to English. *The Prague Bulletin of Mathematical Linguistics*, *91*, 57-66.

Welsh Government (2019) 2050: A million Welsh speakers. Annual report 2017–18. Available at: https://gov.wales/sites/default/files/publications/2019-03/cymraeg-2050-a-million-welsh-speakers-annual-report-2017-18.pdf Retrieved: [02/07/2019].

Adapting Term Recognition to an Under-Resourced Language: the Case of Irish

John P. McCrae
Insight Centre for Data Analytics
Data Science Institute
National University of Ireland Galway
`john@mccr.ae`

Adrian Doyle
National University of Ireland Galway
`A.DOYLE35@nuigalway.ie`

Abstract

Automatic Term Recognition (ATR) is an important method for the summarization and analysis of large corpora, and normally requires a significant amount of linguistic input, in particular the use of part-of-speech taggers. For an under-resourced language such as Irish, the resources necessary for this may be scarce or entirely absent. We evaluate two methods for the automatic extraction of terms, based on the small part-of-speech-tagged corpora that are available for Irish and on a large terminology list, and show that both methods can produce viable term extractors. We evaluate this with a newly constructed corpus that is the first available corpus for term extraction in Irish. Our results shine some light on the challenge of adapting natural language processing systems to under-resourced scenarios.

1 Introduction

Automatic term recognition (ATR) is the task of identifying relevant and interesting terms from a text corpus. This can be useful for a wide range of text understanding tasks, however most of the work on this task has to date focused on term extraction for English. In contrast, there are up to 7,000 languages spoken in the world, most of which are severely under-resourced, and the task of adapting Natural Language Processing (NLP) tools to such languages is still not well explored. The principle issue for these language is the lack of resources available and as such they are called *under-resourced languages*. In this paper, we will focus on the development of automatic term recognition for the Irish language, an under-resourced Celtic language spoken primarily on the island of Ireland. In particular, we will base our work on the previously developed Saffron system (Bordea et al., 2014; Pereira et al., 2019). The main requirements for this are the development of a part-of-speech tagger, a lemmatizer and a large background corpus and we will detail in this paper how we constructed these models for Irish.

In particular, the largest challenge was the construction of a part-of-speech tagger and we base our work on two main systems that have been developed based on annotated corpora. Firstly, we look at the system of Uí Dhonnchadha and van Genabith (2006), which was developed on a general language domain and secondly we refer to the system of Lynn et al. (2015), which was developed specifically for tweets. We then looked at an alternative approach using the terminology database, Tearma[1], to provide an annotation over the Irish Wikipedia, 'An Vicipéid'[2]. For both the systems trained on part-of-speech corpora and those on the terminology database, we compare them for the challenge of recognizing terms. We show how we incorporate into our term recognition system morphology information extracted from Pota Focal (Měchura, 2018). To analyse this we developed a small gold standard dataset of Wikipedia articles and compared the two methods on this dataset[3]. We then describe the construction of the automatic

© 2019 The authors. This article is licensed under a Creative Commons 4.0 licence, no derivative works, attribution, CC-BY-ND.

---

[1] `https://www.tearma.ie/eolas/tionscadal.en`

[2] `https://ga.wikipedia.org/wiki/Pr\%C3\%ADomhleathanach`

[3] Datasets and code developed in this work are available at `https://github.com/jmccrae/irish_saffron`

term recognition system and compare the results of these two methods on a small corpus of discussion related to the future of the National University of Ireland Galway. Our results show that both methods provide a viable method of constructing a term extraction system, however there is still a need for significant language specific knowledge in the development of such a system and that new generic methods would be necessary to scale this to more under-resourced languages.

2 Related Work

Automatic term recognition is an area that has seen interest for a long time (Kageura and Umino, 1996), and a number of supervised and unsupervised methods have been proposed. More recently this has led to a couple of mature toolkits for this including Jate (Zhang et al., 2016), ATR4S (Astrakhantsev, 2018) and Saffron (Pereira et al., 2019), the latter of which we use as the basis for this work. This work has been characterized in terms of filters that extract terms, either in terms of 'closed' filters that focus only on nouns (Arora et al., 2014) and open filters that include adjectives (such as in this work). Open filters capture more general terms consisting of adjective and nouns such as 'natural language processing', which cannot be captured by closed filters, which would only accept noun terms such as 'language processing'. The result of choosing an open filter is a trade-off that increases the recall of the system at the cost of precision. Thus, in order to ensure high-quality results, there are a number of methods of ranking that are performed in order to rank the terms and thus to improve the precision of the top ranked candidates. The initial methods in this area focused on the use of term frequency statistics such as TF IDF (Evans and Lefferts, 1995), or the relative frequency of the term compared to a background corpus (Ahmad et al., 1999; Peñas et al., 2001; Church and Gale, 1999). A further approach has been based on the analysis of the term, and in particular the presence of subterms in the same domain, which can be indicative of termhood (Buitelaar et al., 2013). It has been shown that the best performance is generally obtained through a combination of these methods (Astrakhantsev, 2018).

3 Methodology

The methodology for automatic term extraction as implemented by the Saffron system consists of the following steps

1. Part-of-speech tagging is applied to the text corpus.

2. The candidate terms are extracted using a simple regular expression over the part-of-speech tags. For English texts tagged with the Penn Treebank, this was `((NN|JJ|NNP|NNS)+(IN|NN|JJ|NNP|NNS)*)?(NN|CD|NNS)`

3. A morphological engine is used to create a single normalized base form for the term, e.g., in English we turn plural nouns into singular nouns.

4. The frequency of the terms is recorded and from this a number of metrics are calculated (see Section 3.4).

5. The candidates are ranked according to the mean reciprocal rank of the metrics and top N candidates are returned.

From this it can be seen the key language-dependent elements are: part-of-speech tagging, term normalization and the inclusion of a background corpus for some of the metrics. We will explain how we adapted this procedure to Irish.

3.1 Morphology

Irish morphology is noticeably more complex than that of English and this presents a challenge for processing the language that should generally require more resources. For automatic term recognition it is not in general necessary to consider verbs as they do not generally occur in terms, which in the context of Irish is beneficial as verbal morphology is more complex than nominal morphology. On the other hand, verbal morphology is generally regular in Irish, whereas nominal morphology is mostly irregular with plural and genitive forms not generally being predictable from the lemma. As such, the only high accuracy approach to handling Irish nominal morphology is a dictionary approach and for this we used the Pota Focal dictionary (Měchura, 2018), as it provides an easy to parse XML version of the morphology for the basic vocabulary of the language. In total there are 4,245 lemmas (of which 3,488 are nouns) in Pota Focal, which we used in this work.

dia (7,747)	dé (14,450)	déithe (400)
dhia (2,671)	dhé (83)	dhéithe (59)
ndia (231)	ndé (33)	ndéithe (157)
ollscoil (4,189)	ollscoile (1,141)	ollscoileanna (265)
hollscoil (106)	hollscoile (1,438)	hollscoileanna (234)
n-ollscoil (7)	n-ollscoile (2)	n-ollscoileanna (41)
t-ollscoil (0)*	t-ollscoile (0)*	t-ollscoileanna (0)*

Table 1: Example of the forms that are lemmatized to 'dia' (god) and 'ollscoil' (university) and their frequency in the New Corpus for Ireland. *Ungrammatical forms.

However, a particular challenge with Irish (along with other Celtic languages) is initial mutation, that is the changing of initial consonant by lenition, eclipsis or prefixing of a consonant to a word starting with a vowel. We used hard-coded rules to generate the forms of each word with initial mutation as they were not included in Pota Focal directly, but could be easily and systematically derived. We over-generate forms including applying a t-prefix to feminine nouns such as 'ollscoil', on the principle that it is unlikely that we will generate any errors from recognizing too many forms of the noun. An example of all the forms is given in Table 1 and we give the frequency of each form in the New Corpus for Ireland (Kilgarriff et al., 2006), showing that all forms do occur in text, even those that may be considered ungrammatical. The morphology engine is then implemented by a simple lookup.

3.2 Part-of-speech Tagging

Corpus	Documents	Words	#POS
Uí Dhonnchadha	42	63,096	16
Lynn	3,032	52,279	22

Table 2: Analysis of part-of-speech Corpora used in this work. #POS refers to the number of distinct top-level part of speech categories.

The most important step for the creation of the tool is the identification of terms from the text and this is achieved in English by means of a regular expression over the output of a part-of-speech tagger. For adapting this to Irish, there is the obvious challenge that there is much less available training data for a part-of-speech tagger and secondly that the part-of-speech tagset would naturally differ from that of English, as for example there is no tag for genitive noun in English. To our knowledge there are two part-of-speech corpora available for

Irish of sufficient size to apply machine learning techniques. The first one is from Uí Dhonnchadha and van Genabith (2006) and this corpus consists of the annotation of a number of documents, while a more recent corpus is due to Lynn et al. (2015) and this was created on Twitter by annotating a number of tweets. The basic statistics of the two corpora are given in Table 2, and we can see that both corpora are similar in size (number of words) but there are differences in the number of documents due to the nature of the annotation as in the case of Lynn's corpus each tweet is considered a single document. Uí Dhonnchadha's corpus has more detailed part-of-speech types, however for the purpose of this work we consider only the top category part-of-speechs (e.g., 'noun', 'verb'). In order to adapt our ATR system to this task we further aligned the two corpora to use a single part-of-speech tagging using the following categories: **N**oun, **V**erb, **A**djective, Adverb, Preposition, Conjunction, **P**ronoun, Particle, **D**eterminer and demonstrative[4], Nu**m**eral and **O**ther[5]. Further, we considered verbal nouns as verbs as we do not wish them to be extracted as terms, however we note that this could cause issues as there are many cases where there would be ambiguity between nouns and verbal nouns, for example 'aistriú' means 'translation' as a noun, but 'moving' or 'translating' as a verbal noun. We expect that the original corpora have made this distinction consistently so as to enable ATR, but this is certainly an aspect that deserves further investigation. As such we can use the following regular expression to identify terms

---

[4] Actually determiners (e.g., 'an', 'na') and demonstratives (e.g., 'seo', 'sin', 'úd') are clearly distinct in Irish grammar also determiners, as determiners precede the noun and demonstratives follows the noun. In Uí Dhonnchadha's corpus they are distinct but Lynn confounds them, as such this was the only major failing in harmonizing the two tagsets.

[5] We merged many of Lynn's categories into this category as they were specific to Twitter, e.g., Lynn has two tags for hashtags.

in the text:

```
N ( (N|A|D) * (N|A) +) ?
```

Note that this expression allows an article to occur in the middle of a term, which is quite common in Irish, for example in 'Banc na hÉireaan' (Bank of Ireland). In addition, we observe that it is common for terms in Irish to either start with an article, for example 'An Fhrainc' (France) or contain a preposition, such as 'aistriú focal ar fhocal' (translating word by word), however initial experiments suggested that including prepositions in the pattern lead to too many false positive terms.

3.3 Weak Supervision

While the part-of-speech tagging approach described above has been successful in English and our results show that it is an effective method also for Irish, there are some clear shortcomings of the approach. In particular, the corpora we train on are quite small and as such there is a necessity to make trade-offs for part-of-speech tags that rarely occur within a term. As an alternative, we considered the use of a large database on known terms which exists in the form of the Tearma database. As such we attempted to train a model that could work at identifying terms in context. To achieve this we collected a large corpus of Irish from the Irish Wikipedia, which was selected due to its size and availability but also due to its technical nature meaning that it is likely to contain the terms used in a similar manner to the Tearma database. We used the dump from April 2019 and in total we extracted 10,074 articles totalling 4,093,665 words and we identified all terms from the Tearma database that occur in this corpus of which we found 24,038 terms. We trained our tagging model based on a simple **IOB** tagging (Ramshaw and Marcus, 1999) where a word was tagged as **B** if it was first word from a term, **I** if it occurred in a non-initial position in term and **O** and if it was not in a term in the Tearma database. This naturally leads to a large number of false negatives as many terms that are used in An Vicipéid are not in Tearma, more concerningly we also found a large number of false positives as there were terms in the database that were similar to other common words. An example of this was 'IS', which is an abbreviation for 'Intleacht Shaorga' (Artificial Intelligence), but also matched a very common form of the copula. As such we also filtered the term database as follows:

- If the term occurred more than 3,000 times (this value was hand-tuned) in the corpus it was rejected,

- If the term occurred more than 100 times in the corpus it was accepted only if the first word was marked as a noun in Pota Focal,

- If the term occurred less than 100 times it was accepted as a term.

We also converted the corpora of Uí Dhonnchadha and Lynn to the IOB format so that we could compare the result.

3.4 Term Ranking

The goal of the previous task was to identify candidate terms from the text, and the next step is normally to provide a ranking of these terms so that those which are most relevant to the domain can be identified. A first step is then to provide some basic filters to remove some incorrect terms. In particular, we do the following:

- Filter by the length of the term (up to a maximum of 4 words)

- Remove all terms that consist solely of stopwords[6].

- Has a minimum number of occurrences in the corpus. However, given the size of the corpus we had, this number was set to 1, and so effectively this filter was ignored

We then carried out the scoring of each term according to multiple metrics, this has been shown in previous work (Astrakhantsev, 2018) to be very effective and allows the method to be adjusted to the task. To this extent, we consider a corpus, C, and consider $t \in C$ to a term extracted in the first step. Then, we develop a number of functions $f_i : T \to \mathbb{R}$ that produce a score for this.

We can broadly group the ranking categories into four categories:

3.4.1 Frequency of Occurrences

These methods consider as primary evidence the frequency and distribution of the words, in particular focusing on words that are prevalent in only a few documents in the corpus. We define as usual

---

[6]This proved very useful as the system was lemmatizing 'bhfuil' (a form of the verb 'bí', to be) as 'fuil' (blood)

a set of documents, D, and for each word a frequency across all documents denoted, $tf(w)$. We can then define document frequency, $df(w)$, as the number of documents, $d \in D$, where the word occurs at least once. We can then define the following basic metrics:

Total TF-IDF is a well-established method for estimating the importance of a term based on how frequently occurs but penalizing terms that occur uniformly across the corpus.

$$\text{Total TF-IDF}(w) = tf(w) \log \left(\frac{|D|}{df(w)} \right)$$

Residual IDF (Church and Gale, 1995) compares the distribution of TF-IDF against an expectancy of it being randomly distributed.

$$\text{Residual IDF}(w) = tf(w) \times$$
$$\left[\log_2 \left(1 - \exp \left(\frac{tf(w)}{|D|} \right) \right) - \log_2 \left(\frac{df(w)}{|D|} \right) \right]$$

3.4.2 Context of occurrences

These functions incorporate the distributional hypothesis (Harris, 1954), by including information about how terms occur within other terms. For this we define $T_{sub}(w)$ as the set of terms which are contained in w, that is all sub-sequences of the words of w and $T_{super}(w)$ as all terms that contain w occurring in the corpus. We can then defined the following metrics:

Combo Basic (Astrakhantsev, 2015) uses the count of both the super- and subterms as well as the length (in words) of the term, $|w|$:

$$\text{ComboBasic}(w) = |w| tf(w) +$$
$$\alpha |T_{super}(w)| + \beta |T_{sub}(w)|$$

Similarly, cValue (Ananiadou, 1994) uses the subterm frequency as well:

$$\text{cValue}(w) = \log_2(|w| + 0.1) \times$$
$$\left(tf(w) - \frac{\sum_{t' \in T_{sub}(w)} tf(t')}{|T_{sub}(w)|} \right)$$

The domain coherence measures the correlation, using probabilistic mutual information, of the term with other words in the corpus and then uses this to predict a score, in particular we use the PostRankDC method (Buitelaar et al., 2013).

3.4.3 Reference Corpora

Another important distinguishing factor about terms is that they are very frequent in their domain but not widely used outside that domain. We do measure this by taking a background corpus with term frequencies given as $tf_{ref}(w)$, let $T = \sum_t f(w)$ be the total size in words in the foreground corpus and $T_r ef$ be the total total size of the background corpus. We can define Weirdness (Ahmad et al., 1999) as:

$$\text{Weirdness}(w) = \frac{tf(w)}{tf_{ref}(w)}$$

And a second metric Relevance (Peñas et al., 2001) as:

$$\text{Relevance}(w) = 1 -$$
$$\log \left(2 + \frac{tf(w) T_{ref} df(w)}{tf_{ref} w T |D|} \right)$$

3.4.4 Topic Modelling

Finally, the use of topic models has been suggested based on the success of Latent Dirichlet Allocation (Blei et al., 2003) in the form of the Novel Topic Model (NTM) (Li et al., 2013), although we did not in fact use this metric, as our previous experiments have shown it to perform poorly. NTM requires a probability distribution of a word being labelled to one of K topics, $p(w_i = w | z_i = k)$, the score is then calculated as

$$\text{NTM}(w) = tf(w) \sum_{v \in w} \max_k P(w_i = w | z_i = k)$$

3.4.5 Multi-metric scoring

Once all the scores for all candidate terms have been calculated, a ranking of the top terms is necessary. In general, these terms produce very different scores and as such, methodologies such as linear models (e.g., support vector machines) or simple classifiers (e.g., feed-forward neural networks) would not work well and would require significant training data. Instead, we have observed that the use of the unsupervised methods of *mean reciprocal rank* produces a very strong result without the need for training. For this we produce from each score a ranking function $R_i : T \to \mathbb{N}$ that produces the rank (from 1) of the score and then calculate the final score as:

$$score(t) = \sum_{i}^{n} \frac{1}{R_i(t)} \qquad (1)$$

For our experiments we used a combination of metrics that has proven to work well across many settings that consist of the five scores: ComboBasic, Weirdness, TF-IDF, cValue and Residual IDF. Then we apply a filtering step to select the top n candidates; for our experiments we set $n = 100$.

4 Gold Standard Creation

	B	I	O
Uí Dhonnchadha	22%	17%	61%
Lynn	19%	10%	71%
Tearma	19%	2%	80%
Gold	16%	11%	73%

Table 3: The comparative tagging of each of the corpora using the IOB scheme.

In order to evaluate this approach we manually annotated a small section of the Wikipedia corpus. In total we annotated 11 documents consisting of 5,178 words and found among those 846 terms. This annotation was carried out by a single annotator and while this makes it difficult to estimate the quality of the annotation, this is unfortunately a typical issue with developing resources for under-resourced languages. In Table 3, we see the proportion of words marked with the IOB schema and see that the corpus of Lynn is most similar in terms of composition of the corpus. Moreover, we see that the distant supervision by Tearma while producing a similar ratio of terms, has far fewer words marked as I, suggesting that there are more one-word terms in this corpus than the part-of-speech tagging based corpora. An example of this annotation is given in Figure 1.

5 Results

In order to evaluate the effectiveness of our automatic term recognition approach we evaluated the accuracy of the extraction in various settings. For the part-of-speech-based extraction we considered the two corpora of Uí Dhonnchadha and Lynn separately as well as in a 'merged' mode, where we aligned the part-of-speech tags between the two corpora. We also considered each of these corpora where we converted the tagging from the part-of-speech tags to the IOB scheme and then trained

Is í **an tSomáilis** an **teanga** a labhraíonn formhor*[sic]* muintir **na Somáile** agus na **Somálaigh** sna tíortha in aice láimhe . Is **teanga Cúiseach** í agus í an dara **teanga Cúiseach** is mó a labhraítear ar domhan í (i ndiaidh **na hOraimise**).

Term	Translation
an tSomáilis	Somali (language)
teanga	language
an tSomáil	Somalia
Somálach	Somali (person)
teanga Cúiseach	Cushitic Language
an Oraimis	Oromo

Figure 1: An example from the gold standard annotated corpus with terms in bold and the extracted terms with translations

the model on the IOB tags. In addition, we considered the weakly supervised training scheme by using the Tearma-based model and finally we concatenated all corpora with IOB tags to produce a corpus called 'All'. We trained all models with the OpenNLP toolkit using the standard maximum entropy model[7]. In the case of using the part-of-speech tagged corpora the data was trained using the default parameters of the models and the top-level part-of-speech tags as described in Section 3.2, which for the Tearma database and the models using IOB we again used the default parameters with each word being tagged as either 'I', 'O' or 'B'. We note that the maximum entropy model implemented by OpenNLP is probably not state-of-the-art and does not take advantage of word embeddings or other techniques. This implementation is used by Saffron due to it being a reasonable trade-off between accuracy and computational cost, as well as being openly licensed without any copy-left restrictions, however this will likely be revised in the future. In Table 4 we show the results of the extraction presented in terms of precision, recall and F-Measure on each of the classes. We see that no training corpus performs best on all classes, for the B and I class the part-of-speech based system is best when both corpora are combined with only a minor difference between the part-of-speech tags and the IOB tag scheme. For the O class, however the Tearma corpus performs best, and the effect of adding the part-of-speech tagged corpora seems to be very marginal.

---

[7]As implemented by `POSTaggerME` in OpenNLP

	B			I			O		
	P	R	F	P	R	F	P	R	F
Random (baseline)	0.163	0.163	0.163	0.111	0.111	0.111	0.726	0.726	0.726
Uí Dhonnchadha	0.676	0.458	0.546	**0.777**	0.327	0.460	0.648	0.951	0.771
Lynn	0.707	0.490	0.579	0.739	0.446	0.556	0.759	0.948	0.843
Merged	**0.722**	0.498	0.589	0.747	0.468	**0.576**	0.770	**0.953**	0.851
Uí Dhonnchadha (IOB)	0.656	0.432	0.521	0.725	0.302	0.427	0.625	0.933	0.748
Lynn (IOB)	0.670	0.467	0.551	0.537	0.485	0.510	0.801	0.905	0.850
Merged (IOB)	0.707	0.506	**0.590**	0.681	0.480	0.563	0.790	0.933	0.855
Tearma	0.612	0.506	0.554	0.101	0.806	0.180	0.906	0.834	**0.869**
All	0.618	**0.507**	0.557	0.098	**0.824**	0.174	**0.907**	0.835	**0.869**

Table 4: Per-class performance of term extraction for various training inputs evaluated on the gold standard.

We then ran the full pipeline embedded in the Saffron system and described in Section 3.4, using An Vicipéid as a background corpus. This was applied to a set of chat dialogues that concerned plans for the future of National University of Ireland Galway. Considering each comment as a single document we used a corpus of 239 documents totalling 9,313 words. We considered two of the best scoring settings for this from the previous experiment and the top 20 extracted terms for each settings are shown in Table 5.

6 Discussion

The results presented show that both the extraction using a part-of-speech tagged corpus and using the weak supervision by using a term database can be effective at developing a term extraction system. The principle difference can be seen from the corpus, in that the Tearma based approach extracted many more one word terms than the part-of-speech-based approach, and this is probably due to the inclusion of many short words as terms, that may have a specific meaning as domain terminology but are also frequently used in general. This can be seen from the higher prevalence of the 'B' tag in Table 3 and by the comparatively better performance on the 'O' class on the gold standard in Table 4. This is further clearer in the top 20 extracted terms in Table 5, where we can see that the Tearma based system extracted many more one-word terms but only extracted one multiword term (excluding those terms that erroneously contain the definite article 'an'). However, the corpus developed by the Tearma approach was much larger than that which has part-of-speech tags, so performance of this methodology may be impaired.

As such, it seems clear that both methods are viable approaches and in the context of an under-resourced language both options could be used as the basis for creating a term extractor. As the list of terms is a resource that in general requires less specialist expertise to be created and may be more available for languages with even fewer resources than Irish, for example by using the page titles of Wikipedia articles, it is good to see that for the task of automatic term recognition it may not be necessary to engage in the expensive process of annotating a corpus with part-of-speech tags. That said, given the relatively small size of the part-of-speech tagged corpus, it may follow that effort spent here more directly translates into improvement in the quality of automatic term recognition.

We were not able to provide a good quantitative evaluation of the quality of the extracted terms as this would require a significant and costly analysis of the corpus as well as creating a ranked list of highly relevant terms that is difficult to achieve. However we have provided the top 20 terms in Table 5, and will provide a qualitative evaluation of them here. Both lists contain a similar number of non-terms (four each). This is also based on the assumption that 'déan' is an error, which while a very relevant term in this context, referring back to the corpus suggests that this was actually a from of the verb, e.g., the verbal noun 'déanamh', and so should not have been extracted, a similar case may apply to 'úsáid' which can be both a noun and a verbal noun. In much the same way, it seems that 'cónaí' was entirely used in the phrase 'i gcónaí' (always) rather than as an independent term. Moreover, there are a number of errors in the lemmatization in both lists in particular with relation to the rather specialized term 'ollscolaíocht', which does not occur in Pota Focal. Also, in a few

Part-of-speech		Tearma	
Irish	Translation	Irish	Translation
gaeilge	Irish	ollscoil	university
mac léinn	student	foireann	staff
ollscoil	university	ceart	right
ionad ghaeltachta	Irish centre	an phobail†	the public
teanga	language	dátheangach	bilingual
duine	person	obair	work
mac	son	cúrsa	course
scéim teanga	language plan	seirbhís	service
gaeltacht	Irish-speaking area	ceist	question
foireann na hollscoile	university staff	bliain	year
pobal	public	deis	opportunity
áras na gaeilge	Irish Building at NUIG	easpa ceannaireachta	lack of leadership
pobal na hollscoile	people of the university	leanúnach	successor
léann	learning	*déan*	dean/'to do'
foireann	staff	iarraidh	request
cuid na hollscoile	part of the university	oifigeach	officer
níos mó	more	dualgas	duty
meán	media	*cónaí*	residence/always
cúrsa	course	pleán†	plan
leath na gaeilge	for Irish	scéim	plan
hOllscolaíochta gaeilge†	Irish Language University Education	comhrá	conversation
seirbhís	service	úsáid	usage
cónaí	residence/always	*inbhuanaithe*	sustainable
deis	opportunity	cultúr	culture
ball foirne	member of stafff	an gclár†	the programme
oifigeach na gaeilge	Irish language officer	plean	plan
hOllscolaíochta †	university education	*an rud*	the thing
oifigeach	officer	ról	role
ceist	question	oideachas	education
acadamh na hóige	youth academy	an domhan	the world

Table 5: The Top 20 ranked terms extracted using the part-of-speech tagged corpus and the distant supervision via Tearma. Italics indicate terms that are likely incorrect terms, † indicates terms with a lemmatization issues.

cases, we see terms that were extracted were possibly also used as adjectives, and hence would not be terms, in particular 'dátheangach' and 'leanúnach', which are very rarely used as a noun. Finally, we note that the Tearma-based system extracted the spelling error '*plean' (which should likely be 'plean'), which while incorrect is interesting given that this misspelled form did not occur in training suggesting that the system has been able to generalize effectively.

7   Conclusion

We have analyzed two methods for the construction of an automated term recognition system for an under-resourced language. We have found that both methods make effective methods for training a system that is significantly better than a random baseline, however our analysis shows that there are still weaknesses with each system, suggesting that performance is being limited by the availability of resources. Further, it seems that basic linguistic facts such as the length of the term are being affected by the the resources and methods we are using to create the system and this could be a focus of further study.

Acknowledgements

This publication has emanated from research supported in part by a research grant from Science Foundation Ireland (SFI) under Grant Number SFI/12/RC/2289, co-funded by the European Regional Development Fund, and the European Unions Horizon 2020 research and innovation programme under grant agreement No 731015, ELEXIS - European Lexical Infrastructure and grant agreement No 825182, Prêt-à-LLOD.

References

Ahmad, Khurshid, Lee Gillam, Lena Tostevin, et al. 1999. University of Surrey Participation in TREC8: Weirdness Indexing for Logical Document Extrapolation and Retrieval (WILDER). In *TREC*, pages 1–8.

Ananiadou, Sophia. 1994. A methodology for automatic term recognition. In *COLING 1994 Volume 2: The 15th International Conference on Computational Linguistics*, volume 2.

Arora, Chetan, Mehrdad Sabetzadeh, Lionel Briand, and Frank Zimmer. 2014. Improving requirements glossary construction via clustering: approach and industrial case studies. In *Proceedings of the 8th ACM/IEEE International Symposium on Empirical Software Engineering and Measurement*, page 18. ACM.

Astrakhantsev, Nikita. 2015. *Methods and software for terminology extraction from domain-specific text collection*. Ph.D. thesis, Ph. D. thesis, Institute for System Programming of Russian Academy of Sciences.

Astrakhantsev, Nikita. 2018. ATR4S: toolkit with state-of-the-art automatic terms recognition methods in Scala. *Language Resources and Evaluation*, 52(3):853–872.

Blei, David M, Andrew Y Ng, and Michael I Jordan. 2003. Latent Dirichlet allocation. *Journal of Machine Learning Research*, 3:993–1022.

Bordea, Georgeta, Paul Buitelaar, and Barry Coughlan. 2014. Hot Topics and schisms in NLP: Community and Trend Analysis with Saffron on ACL and LREC Proceedings. In *Proceedings of the Ninth LREC, Reykjavik, Iceland, ACL Anthology: L14-1697*.

Buitelaar, Paul, Georgeta Bordea, and Tamara Polajnar. 2013. Domain-independent term extraction through domain modelling. In *The 10th international conference on terminology and artificial intelligence (TIA 2013), Paris, France*. 10th International Conference on Terminology and Artificial Intelligence.

Church, Kenneth W and William A Gale. 1995. Poisson mixtures. *Natural Language Engineering*, 1(2):163–190.

Church, Kenneth and William Gale. 1999. Inverse document frequency (IDF): A measure of deviations from Poisson. In *Natural language processing using very large corpora*, pages 283–295. Springer.

Evans, David A and Robert G Lefferts. 1995. CLARIT-TREC experiments. *Information processing & management*, 31(3):385–395.

Harris, Zellig S. 1954. Distributional structure. *Word*, 10(2-3):146–162.

Kageura, Kyo and Bin Umino. 1996. Methods of automatic term recognition: A review. *Terminology. International Journal of Theoretical and Applied Issues in Specialized Communication*, 3(2):259–289.

Kilgarriff, Adam, Michael Rundell, and Elaine Uí Dhonnchadha. 2006. Efficient corpus development for lexicography: building the New Corpus for Ireland. *Language resources and evaluation*, 40(2):127–152.

Li, Sujian, Jiwei Li, Tao Song, Wenjie Li, and Baobao Chang. 2013. A novel topic model for automatic term extraction. In *Proceedings of the 36th international ACM SIGIR conference on Research and development in information retrieval*, pages 885–888. ACM.

Lynn, Teresa, Kevin Scannell, and Eimear Maguire. 2015. Minority language Twitter: Part-of-speech tagging and analysis of Irish tweets. In *Proceedings of the Workshop on Noisy User-generated Text*, pages 1–8.

Měchura, Michal Boleslav. 2018. Maidir le Pota Focal. URL: `http://www.potafocal.com/_info/`.

Peñas, Anselmo, Felisa Verdejo, Julio Gonzalo, et al. 2001. Corpus-based terminology extraction applied to information access. In *Proceedings of Corpus Linguistics*, volume 2001, page 458. Citeseer.

Pereira, Bianca, Cecile Robin, Tobias Daudert, John P. McCrae, and Paul Buitelaar. 2019. Taxonomy Extraction for Customer Service Knowledge Base Construction. In *Submitted to SEMANTICS 2019*.

Ramshaw, Lance A and Mitchell P Marcus. 1999. Text chunking using transformation-based learning. In *Natural language processing using very large corpora*, pages 157–176. Springer.

Uí Dhonnchadha, Elaine and Josef van Genabith. 2006. A Part-of-Speech tagger for Irish using finite state morphology and constraint grammar disambiguation.

Zhang, Ziqi, Jie Gao, and Fabio Ciravegna. 2016.
JATE 2.0: Java Automatic Term Extraction with
Apache Solr. In *Proceedings of the 10th edition of
the Language Resources and Evaluation Conference
(LREC)*.

Leveraging backtranslation to improve machine translation for Gaelic languages

Meghan Dowling
ADAPT Centre
Dublin City University

Teresa Lynn
ADAPT Centre
Dublin City University

Andy Way
ADAPT Centre
Dublin City University

`firstname.lastname@adaptcentre.ie`

Abstract

Irish and Scottish Gaelic are similar but distinct languages from the Celtic language family. Both languages are under-resourced in terms of machine translation (MT), with Irish being the better resourced. In this paper, we show how backtranslation can be used to harness the resources of these similar low-resourced languages and build a Scottish-Gaelic to English MT system with little or no high-quality bilingual data.

1 Introduction

Irish (GA) and Scottish Gaelic (GD) are recognised minority languages, both in their native countries and in the EU. Both languages are minority languages, with English (EN) as the dominant language. Irish is also the first official language of Ireland and an official EU language. This benefits the Irish language in terms of MT resources because a certain amount of public information is required by law to be available in Irish, both at a national and European level[1]. Although Scottish Gaelic is recognised in the UK by the Gaelic Language Act (2005)[2], neither the UK government nor the EU are legally obliged to publish Scottish Gaelic texts. This has led to a shortage in available corpora suitable for training statistical machine translation (SMT) and neural machine translation (NMT) systems. Without the support of laws that require the output of Scottish Gaelic content, there is the risk that GD MT will not be able to reach the same status as other major languages.

As with other low-resourced and inflected languages, Gaelic languages suffer from data sparsity. While other language pairs can achieve high translation accuracy using state-of-the-art data-hungry methods, language pairs with fewer resources often have to employ creative methods to improve MT quality. One such approach is to create artificial data to boost the amount of corpora available for training. The premise of this method is that even if the data is not of a high quality, the MT system can still draw benefits from the extra data. Backtranslation is one such method for increasing the amount of creating artificial data. This paper describes our efforts to, through backtranslation, leverage the greater number of language resources available to Irish to improve MT systems for GD↔GA and GD↔EN.

This paper is laid out as follows: Section 2 and Section 3 give some background in terms of MT and linguistics. The data used in these experiments is detailed in Section 4. Section 5 describes the methodology employed in these experiments, the results of which are presented and discussed in Section 6. Finally, some avenues for future work are described in Section 7.

2 MT background

Data sparsity in low-resourced languages is exacerbated by the advent of NMT (Sutskever et al., 2014; Bahdanau et al., 2015), a data-hungry MT paradigm that requires huge amounts of parallel text to train a system of sufficient quality.[3] We be-

© 2019 The authors. This article is licensed under a Creative Commons 4.0 licence, no derivative works, attribution, CC-BY-ND.

[1]There is currently a derogation in place within the EU which restricts the amount of content required to be translated to Irish. This is due to lift at the end of 2021.

[2]`https://www.legislation.gov.uk/asp/2005/7/contents`

[3]A marker of sufficient quality could be taken from Escartín and Arcedillo (2015) who indicate that a BLEU score of 45+ can increase translator productivity for EN-ES.

lieve that language technology resources are vital for the preservation and growth of every language and that it is necessary to develop methods of creating MT systems for languages without an extensive amount of language data available.

Previous experiments have shown backtranslation to be a viable method of artificial data creation (Sennrich et al., 2015; Burlot and Yvon, 2018; Poncelas et al., 2018). One possible benefit of backtranslation is that it allows the use of more than one MT paradigm (e.g. rule-based, statistical, neural) to create a MT model. In this way, the resulting model could gain benefits from each paradigm used.

Apertium (Forcada et al., 2011) is an open source machine translation platform which uses rule-based machine translation (RBMT) as the underlying MT technology. One of the benefits of RBMT is that it requires no parallel data, apart from a dictionary. There have been some efforts towards creating a RBMT system for GA↔GD. However, the GA↔GD Apertium module is listed as being in the *incubator* stage, which indicates that more work is needed before the MT system can be classed as being reliable.

There has been some previous work to create a GA→GD MT system with little or no data (Scannell, 2006). In this approach, the author builds a pipeline-style MT system which uses stages of standardisation, part-of-speech tagging, word sense disambiguation, syntactic transfer, lexical transfer and post-processing. There is also some literature surrounding the development of a SMT system for the GA–GD pair (Scannell, 2014). This approach involves training a word-based model, similar to the IBM model 1.

Research has been carried out on GD-EN NMT (Chen, 2018), in which the author uses linguistic features such as glosses to improve the system.

3 Linguistic overview

Translating between sentences with differing sentence structures can be a challenge for MT systems and can lead to poor quality MT output, particularly for longer sentences (Koehn and Knowles, 2017). Gaelic languages employ a verb-subject-object (VSO) sentence structure, different to the sentence-verb-object (SVO) structure more commonly seen in Indo-European languages. Figure 1 illustrates the similar word order of Scottish Gaelic and Irish, and how it diverges with that of English.

GD: Chuala e stòraidh ùr
GA: Chuala sé scéal nua
EN: He heard a new story

Figure 1: An example sentence highlighting the divergent word order between English and both Irish and Gaelic

Irish and Scottish Gaelic both display richer morphology than English. Example sentence 1 shows the inflection of the feminine nouns *'creag'* (GD) and *'carraig'* (GA), both meaning 'rock' or 'cliff'[4]. Inflection can have an impact on data sparsity (inflected words seen less frequently in training data) and also on automatic evaluation metrics such as BLEU (Papineni et al., 2002), which considers inflected words as being wholly different from their uninflected counterparts, and can sometimes penalise translation output too harshly as a result (Callison-Burch et al., 2006).

(1)	*creag*	rock/a rock	*carraig*
	a' chreag	the rock	*an charraig*
	creagan	rocks	carraig**eacha**
	na creige	of the rock	*na carraige*

4 Data

SMT and NMT, currently the two most prominent MT paradigms, require large amounts of bilingual data. Therefore, the availability of data plays a huge part in the quality of MT output. In this section we describe the GD and GA language data resources used in our experiments.

4.1 Scottish Gaelic

Wikipedia Scottish Gaelic language Wikipedia (Uicipeid[5]) contains 14,801 articles at the time of download [6]. Pre-processing including sentence tokenising, removal of wiki-text, tags and blank lines was performed, providing us with a resulting corpus of 87,788 sentences of monolingual Scottish Gaelic. This corpus can be described as being of mixed domain, with clear, formal sentences.

OPUS OPUS (Tiedemann, 2012) is a repository of language resources available for download from

---

[4]For clarity, the inflection markers (letters) in each example are displayed in bold
[5]https://gd.wikipedia.org
[6]04/04/2019

the web[7]. OPUS provides us with bilingual GA–GD and EN-GD corpora from a number of sources. Two bilingual GA–GD corpora that OPUS provides us with are the Ubuntu (655 parallel sentences) and GNOME (5,317 sentences) manuals. These are strictly within the technical domain, and often contain 'sentences' that are in fact 1-3 word phrases rich in technical jargon. Tatoeba, another OPUS source, is a corpus of short, simplified sentences for language learning purposes. While there was not a GD–GA Tatoeba corpus available, we downloaded the monolingual corpora for each language and manually aligned any matching sentences (referred to as Tatoeba-ga). OPUS also provides us with EN-GD parallel corpora from Tatoeba (Tatoeba-en), Ubuntu and GNOME.

4.2 Irish

In this work, we use the datasets described by Dowling et al. (2018). This consists of 108,000 parallel sentences from sources such as the Department of Culture, Heritage and the Gaeltacht and the Citizens Information website[8].

Corpus	# GA words	# GD words	# EN words
Uicipeid	N/A	1,449,636	N/A
Ubuntu	20,166	25,125	N/A
GNOME	14,897	19,956	N/A
Tatoeba-ga	466	489	N/A
Tatoeba-en	N/A	2,556	2,254
EN–GA	1,859,042	N/A	1,697,387
TOTAL	**1,894,571**	**1,497,762**	**1,699,641**

Table 1: Number of words in bilingual (GD-EN, GD-GA, GA-EN) and monolingual (GD only) corpora used

5 Method

In these experiments we take an approach to building an MT system using backtranslation illustrated by Figure 2. In step (1) monolingual data in language X (e.g. GA) is translated to language Y (e.g. GD) using the Apertium RBMT system. This creates an artificial parallel dataset. In step (2) this artificial dataset is then used to train a SMT system in the opposite language direction (e.g. GD→GA). (3) The resulting system can be used to translate new documents from language Y to language X.

[7]http://opus.nlpl.eu/
[8]https://www.citizensinformation.ie

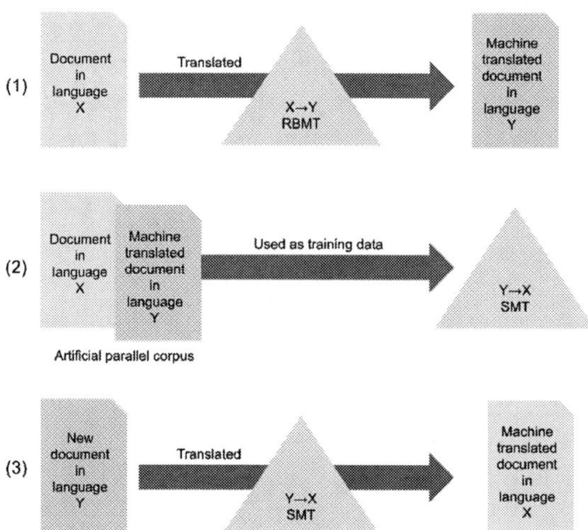

Figure 2: Simplified diagram of backtranslation method used to build SMT systems in these experiments

We carry out four sets of experiments (1, 2, 3 and 4) based on each language pair.

Experiment 1: GD→GA   In these experiments (1A–C in Table 2), the Ubuntu and GNOME data sets are used as the authentic training data and the Uicipeid dataset is used as the basis of the artificial bilingual dataset (see Section 4).

Experiment 2: GA→GD   To maintain consistency, the authentic dataset used in Exp. 1 is also used in these experiments (2A–C in Table 2). The bilingual artificial dataset is generated through backtranslation of the GA dataset used in previous EN-GA research, as described in Section 4.2.

Experiment 3: GD→EN   With a relatively large EN-GA parallel dataset at our disposal, we chose to take this backtranslation method a step further. In these experiments (3A–C in Table 2), the GA side of the EN-GA dataset is translated to Scottish Gaelic using Apertium, as in 5. However, rather than pairing the machine translated Scottish Gaelic text with the authentic Irish text, we instead choose to train a system using the EN portion of the authentic EN-GA dataset. This results in a GD→EN SMT system.

Experiment 4: EN→GD   The method of generating artificial corpora is identical to that of Exp. 3, with the exception of the change in language direction. The results for these experiments are presented as experiments 4A–C in Table 2.

5.1 Building and adding to the baseline

Each experiment contains three parts (referred to in Table 2). Part **A** involves creating a baseline by training a SMT system using only authentic data. Part **B** trains a SMT system using the artificial dataset created through backtranslation. This experiment most closely resembles Figure 2. Finally, in part **C**, the authentic and artificial datasets are combined to train a SMT system. Systems are trained using Moses (Koehn et al., 2007) with default parameters, with the exception of the GD↔EN systems which use a 6-gram language model and hierarchical reordering tables to partly address the divergent word order between the two languages.

6 Results and Conclusions

We report on BLEU (Papineni et al., 2002), an automatic metric of evaluating MT, to provide an indication of quality for the MT systems trained. For consistency in domain, the test data for all systems comes from the Tatoeba source. It should be noted that while the source is the same, Tateoba-ga and Tatoeba-en differ in both content and size (see Section 4).

Exp.	Auth.	Artif.	Lang.	BLEU
Apert.	N/A	N/A	GA→GD	8.67
1A	5,645	0	GA→GD	12.43
1B	0	87,788	GA→GD	16.63
1C	5,645	87,788	GA→GD	**25.45**
Apert.	N/A	N/A	GA→GD	13.73
2A	5,645	0	GD→GA	14.32
2B	0	108,000	GD→GA	17.46
2C	5,645	108,000	GD→GA	**22.55**
3A	18,785	0	GD→EN	3.73
3B	0	108,000	GD→EN	6.53
3C	18,785	108,000	GD→EN	**11.41**
4A	18,785	0	EN→GD	3.05
4B	0	108,000	EN→GD	7.03
4C	18,785	108,000	EN→GD	**10.59**

Table 2: BLEU scores for each experiment (Exp.), with the number of authentic (Auth.) and artificial (Artif.) sentences used to train each system. Scores are also given for the Apertium (Apert.) system used to generate the artificial data.

The results presented in Table 2 and Fig. 3 show a marked improvement in BLEU score over the baseline when backtranslated data is included as training data. We also include BLEU scores for the Apertium GA-GD module, generated through the translation of the test corpus Tatoeba-ga. Despite the low BLEU score of the Apertium GA-GD module, SMT systems trained using solely artificial data also show an increase in BLEU over the baseline. This indicates that even if the quality of the MT system used to backtranslate is poor, it may still be possible to gain benefits from the backtranslated data. The highest automatic scores from all 4 experiment series are produced when the authentic corpus is paired with the artificial data. It is interesting to note that while BLEU scores for the EN↔GD experiments (3A-4C) are substantially lower the same trend can still be seen. This could indicate that backtranslation is a usable method of artificial data creation, even with linguistically different language pairs such as EN–GD.

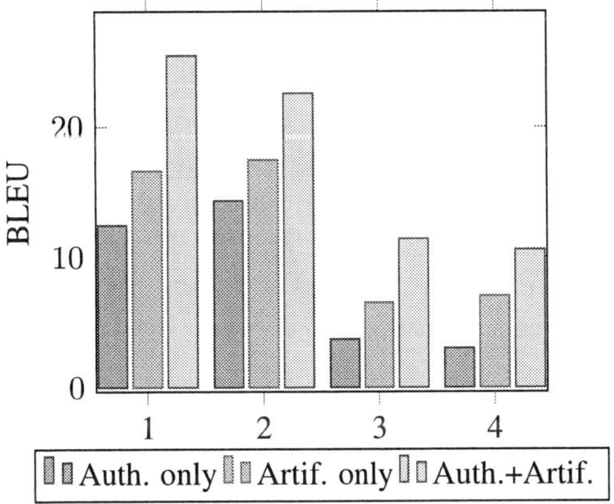

Figure 3: Bar chart of BLEU scores for each experiment. 1, 2, 3 and 4 refer to Experiments 1-4 in Section 5 and Table 2.

7 Future Work

In terms of future work, human analysis will be necessary to determine if there is an actual increase in quality (in terms of usabiltiy, fluency, etc.), rather than relying on automatic metrics.

Another possible avenue for future work is to use a system similar to that of Scannell (2006) to assess whether backtranslated data of a higher quality could be produced, presumably resulting in a more accurate MT output. Furthermore, while GA and GD are generally similar in sentence structure, there are a few cases where the two differ. It would be interesting to observe the standard of MT within these divergent situations and, if the standard is lower, investigate whether the inclusion of linguistic rules such as those used in Scannell (2006) could lead to an increase in quality.

We also note that Tatoeba is a corpus of simple, short sentences. It would be pertinent to repeat these experiments with test data from different domains to investigate if the same increase in BLEU is witnessed with other types of input.

Other monolingual data sources, such as Corpas na Gàidhlig[9] or Irish Wikipedia[10] could be used as sources for the creation of more backtranslated data. It would be interesting to view the effect of additional artificial data on the MT output. Moreover, if a large enough artificial corpus could be generated, these experiments could be repeated with NMT instead of SMT and compared to the research of Chen (2018).

It is our hope that this work could form a basis on which to extend to other Celtic languages and investigate whether it is useful for improving resources for similarly resourced languages.

Acknowledgements

This work is funded by Science Foundation Ireland in the ADAPT Centre (Grant 13/RC/2106) at Dublin City University and partly funded by the Irish Government Department of Culture, Heritage and the Gaeltacht. We thank the reviewers for their valuable comments and advice.

References

Bahdanau, Dzmitry, KyungHyun Cho, and Yoshua Bengio. 2015. Neural machine translation by jointly learning to align and translate. In *Proceedings of International Conference on Learning Representations*.

Burlot, Franck and François Yvon. 2018. Using monolingual data in neural machine translation: a systematic study. In *Proceedings of the Third Conference on Machine Translation: Research Papers*, pages 144–155.

Callison-Burch, Chris, Miles Osborne, and Philipp Koehn. 2006. Re-evaluation the role of bleu in machine translation research. In *11th Conference of the European Chapter of the Association for Computational Linguistics*.

Chen, Yuan-Lu. 2018. *Improving Neural Net Machine Translation Systems with Linguistic Information*. Ph.D. thesis.

Dowling, Meghan, Teresa Lynn, Alberto Poncelas, and Andy Way. 2018. SMT versus NMT: Preliminary comparisons for Irish. In *Proceedings of the AMTA 2018 Workshop on Technologies for MT of Low Resource Languages (LoResMT 2018)*, pages 12–20.

Escartín, Carla Parra and Manuel Arcedillo. 2015. Living on the edge: productivity gain thresholds in machine translation evaluation metrics. In *4th Workshop on Post-Editing Technology and Practice (WPTP4)*, page 46.

Forcada, Mikel L, Mireia Ginestí-Rosell, Jacob Nordfalk, Jim O'Regan, Sergio Ortiz-Rojas, Juan Antonio Pérez-Ortiz, Felipe Sánchez-Martínez, Gema Ramírez-Sánchez, and Francis M Tyers. 2011. Apertium: a free/open-source platform for rule-based machine translation. *Machine translation*, 25(2):127–144.

Koehn, Philipp and Rebecca Knowles. 2017. Six challenges for neural machine translation. In *Proceedings of the First Workshop on Neural Machine Translation*, pages 28–39.

Koehn, Philipp, Hieu Hoang, Alexandra Birch, Chris Callison-Burch, Marcello Federico, Nicola Bertoldi, Brooke Cowan, Wade Shen, Christine Moran, Richard Zens, et al. 2007. Moses: Open source toolkit for statistical machine translation. In *Proceedings of the 45th annual meeting of the ACL on interactive poster and demonstration sessions*, pages 177–180. Association for Computational Linguistics.

Papineni, Kishore, Salim Roukos, Todd Ward, and Wei-Jing Zhu. 2002. BLEU: a method for automatic evaluation of machine translation. In *Proceedings of the 40th annual meeting on association for computational linguistics*, pages 311–318. Association for Computational Linguistics.

Poncelas, Alberto, Dimitar Shterionov, Andy Way, Gideon Maillette de Buy Wenniger, and Peyman Passban. 2018. Investigating backtranslation in neural machine translation. In *21st Annual Conference of the European Association for Machine Translation*, page 249.

Scannell, Kevin P. 2006. Machine translation for closely related language pairs. In *Proceedings of the Workshop Strategies for developing machine translation for minority languages*, pages 103–109. Citeseer.

Scannell, Kevin. 2014. Statistical models for text normalization and machine translation. In *Proceedings of the First Celtic Language Technology Workshop*, pages 33–40.

Sennrich, Rico, Barry Haddow, and Alexandra Birch. 2015. Neural machine translation of rare words with subword units. *arXiv preprint arXiv:1508.07909*.

Sutskever, Ilya, Oriol Vinyals, and Quoc V Le. 2014. Sequence to sequence learning with neural networks. In *Advances in neural information processing systems*, pages 3104–3112.

Tiedemann, Jörg. 2012. Parallel data, tools and interfaces in OPUS. In *LREC*, volume 2012, pages 2214–2218.

---

[9] https://dasg.ac.uk/corpus/
[10] https://ga.wikipedia.org

Improving full-text search results on *dúchas.ie* using language technology

Brian Ó Raghallaigh
Fiontar & Scoil na Gaeilge
Dublin City University
Drumcondra, Dublin 9
Ireland

`brian.oraghallaigh@dcu.ie`

Kevin Scannell
Department of Computer Science
Saint Louis University
220 N. Grand Blvd.
Saint Louis, Missouri 63103-2007

`kscanne@gmail.com`

Meghan Dowling
ADAPT Centre
Dublin City University
Glasnevin, Dublin 9
Ireland

`meghan.dowling@adaptcentre.ie`

[1]Abstract

In this paper, we measure the effectiveness of using language standardisation, lemmatisation, and machine translation to improve full-text search results on *dúchas.ie*, the web interface to the Irish National Folklore Collection. Our focus is the Schools' Collection, a scanned manuscript collection which is being transcribed by members of the public via a crowdsourcing initiative. We show that by applying these technologies to the manuscript page transcriptions, we obtain substantial improvements in search engine recall over a test set of actual user queries, with no appreciable drop in precision. Our results motivate the inclusion of this language technology in the search infrastructure of this folklore resource.

1   Background

This research is motivated by an objective to improve access to the Irish *National Folklore Collection*, one of the largest collections of folklore in Europe, and a collection that contains material in both official languages of Ireland, Irish and English. Our proposition is that the full-text search facility available on the collection's website, *dúchas.ie*,[2] can be enhanced by introducing language technology options. By demonstrating that language standardisation, demutation, lemmatisation, and machine translation technologies can improve information retrieval on the website, this paper supports this proposition and motivates the inclusion of these technologies in the search infrastructure.

1.1   The National Folklore Collection

The Irish *National Folklore Collection* (NFC) is a large archive of folkloristic material collected in Ireland mostly during the 20th century, to which material is still being added. Part of the collection was inscribed into the UNESCO *Memory of the World Register* in September 2017.[3] The NFC, which is located in University College Dublin (UCD), aims to collect, preserve and disseminate the oral tradition of Ireland.[4]

In 2012, the *Dúchas* project was established to digitise the collections of the NFC and publish them online. This project is a partnership

---

[1] © 2019 The authors. This article is licensed under a Creative Commons 4.0 licence, no derivative works, attribution, CCBY-ND.

[2] https://www.duchas.ie/en/
[3] https://en.unesco.org/programme/mow/register
[4] http://www.ucd.ie/irishfolklore/en/

between Dublin City University (DCU) and UCD (Ó Cleircín et al., 2014). The first major NFC collection digitised under the Dúchas project was the *Schools' Collection*. The Schools' Collection is a large collection of folklore stories collected from school children throughout Ireland between 1937 and 1939, as part of a state-sponsored scheme (Ó Catháin, 1988). The collection comprises approximately 740,000 manuscript pages.

Approximately 440,000 pages of the collection were digitised, manually indexed, and made available online on *dúchas.ie* between 2013–16. About 79% of the stories on these pages are in English (348,822 stories) and about 21% are in Irish (95,511 stories). These stories are enriched with various browsable metadata, e.g. title/excerpt, collector, informant, location, language.

Stories in the collection are also indexed by topic. The first part of this work was done during the initial field work. The *Irish Folklore Commission* prepared a guide for teachers participating in the scheme, and this guide was published as a handbook entitled *Irish Folklore and Tradition* (Irish Folklore Commission, 1937). This handbook contained 55 topic headings (e.g. *a collection of riddles*, *local cures*, *the potato-crop*, *festival customs*), and teachers were instructed to collect material under these headings. Following the initial field work, researchers in the Irish Folklore Commission produced a topic-based index of the stories collected as part of the scheme. This paper-based index was based primarily on the 55 general topics from the handbook, but a large number of more specific topic headings (e.g. *Fionn Mac Cumhaill*, *1798*, *warts*) were added, bringing the total number of topics up to *c*.1,700. DCU digitised this index in 2014.

In 2016, using the digitised index and the story titles/excerpts indexed under the Dúchas project, and guided by the *MoTIF Pilot Thesaurus of Irish Folklore* (Ryan, 2015) developed by the Digital Repository of Ireland and the National Library of Ireland, DCU produced a shorter list of 208 standardised topic headings (e.g. *riddles*, *folk medicine*, *potatoes*, *events*), and mapped them to the Schools' Collection stories, resulting in a new index for the Schools' Collection on *dúchas.ie*. This index is a mixture of broad headings (e.g. *supernatural and legendary beings*, *events*, *folk medicine*) and narrow headings (e.g. *banshees*, *Halloween*, *whooping-cough*).

In 2014, to facilitate full-text search of the collection, DCU initiated a project to crowdsource transcriptions of the Schools' Collection manuscript pages using a custom-built web-based application open to anyone (Bhreathnach et al., 2019). This project was conceived, in part, because of the problems associated with performing optical character recognition on the pages of the collection, which contain a mix of handwriting styles, a mix of scripts (i.e. Latin and Insular Celtic), and a mix of languages (i.e. Irish English and prestandard Irish).

The project has been a strong success with uptake amongst members of the public, students and folklore scholars. The transcriptions are generally of good quality and usable, in particular the Irish ones. Light editing is sometimes carried out, but bad transcriptions are rejected. Currently 49% of the English pages (*c*.170,000) and 32% of the Irish pages (*c*.31,000) have been transcribed.[5]

The *dúchas.ie* website handles around 35,000 queries per month including around 16,000 full-text searches of the Schools' Collection transcriptions. All of these queries are logged in a database.

1.2 Irish standardisation

The orthography and grammar of the Irish language was standardised in the middle of the last century with the introduction of the *Caighdeán Oifigiúil* ('Official Standard'), first published in 1958 and revised in 2012 and 2017. Today, the standard form of the language is taught in schools, is used in all modern Irish dictionaries (both print and online), and has been almost universally adopted by the Irish-speaking public when writing the language. The spelling simplifications introduced by the standard cause occasional problems for Irish language technology, such as pairs of words that were distinguished in older orthographies which collapse to the same spelling in the standard (e.g. *fiadhach* ('hunting') and *fiach* ('a raven' or 'a

---

[5] https://www.duchas.ie/en/meitheal/

debt'), both written *fiach* in the standard, or *bádh* ('a bay'), *báidh* ('sympathy, liking'), and *bádhadh* ('drowning'), all three written simply *bá* in the standard). Nevertheless, the overall effect of increased consistency and predictability arising from near-universal adoption of the standard has been a tremendous positive for the development of Irish language technology. It does mean, however, that taggers, parsers, and other NLP (natural language processing) tools developed for processing the standard form of the language fail badly when applied to prestandard texts. In the context of the current paper, the disconnect between the prestandard and standard orthographies makes it extremely difficult for users raised on the standard language to search corpora of prestandard texts such as the Schools' Collection.

An Caighdeánaitheoir ('The Standardiser') is an open source software package for standardising Irish texts, first developed around 2006, and detailed in (Scannell, 2014). The software treats standardisation as a machine translation (MT) problem between closely-related languages, employing a hybrid rule-based and statistical model trained on a large corpus of parallel prestandard and standardised texts (including, for example, many important novels and autobiographies first published in the 1920's and 1930's and manually standardised for a modern readership in recent years). It also attempts to correct misspellings before carrying out standardisation. The standardiser has been deployed by two important lexicographical projects in Ireland, the New English-Irish Dictionary project,[6] and the Royal Irish Academy's *Foclóir Stairiúil na Gaeilge* (Uí Dhonnchadha et al., 2014) to help both lexicographers and end-users search their corpora of prestandard texts more effectively.

1.3 Machine translation for Irish

While the 2012 META-NET study on Irish language technology resources (Judge et al., 2012) deemed Irish-language machine translation as being weak or not supported, in recent years we have witnessed some development in this field. Dowling et al. (2015) describe the development of MT for use within the translation

workflow of an Irish government department, while Arcan et al. (2016) provide results of building a more general domain Irish MT system. Most recently, Dowling et al. (2018) compare the two main MT paradigms: statistical machine translation (SMT) and neural machine translation (NMT). Their results indicate that with a low-resourced language such as Irish, particularly when paired with a language that differs in terms of sentence structure and morphological richness, SMT may provide better results.

Building on this knowledge, we choose to duplicate the SMT system described by Dowling et al. for use in our experiment here. We train a phrase-based SMT system using Moses (Koehn et al., 2007), incorporating hierarchical reordering tables (Galley and Manning, 2008) in an attempt to address the divergent sentence structures (verb-subject-object in Irish, subject-verb-object in English). Our translation model is trained using the same 108,796 sentences of parallel data as in Dowling et al. (2018), coming from a variety of sources such as the Department of Culture, Heritage and the Gaeltacht, Conradh na Gaeilge and Citizens Information. We build a 6-gram, rather than the traditional 3-gram, language model using KenLM (Heafield, 2011) which also aims to reduce any negative impact of the divergent word orders. Our datasets are preprocessed – sentence-tokenised, removal of blank lines, tokenisation of punctuation and truecased – before being translated by the MT system.

2 Methodology

Our principal aim in this paper is to investigate the effectiveness of standardisation and machine translation on the performance of the full-text search engine on *dúchas.ie*. We therefore cast this as an Information Retrieval (IR) problem. To this end, we set up experiments which make use of actual search queries submitted by users of the website, and aim to measure precision and recall of the search engine under various experimental conditions. Lacking a gold-standard corpus of relevant/non-relevant documents with which to measure precision and recall, we instead make use of a subset of the 208 topic labels, described in Section 1.1, attached to the stories in the

---

[6] https://www.focloir.ie/

Schools' Collection to create our own test corpus, as follows.

First, we manually examined the top 10,000 search queries submitted to *dúchas.ie* to date, keeping only the Irish language queries (just over 1,500 of the 10,000). Each of these was then manually compared with the list of 208 standardised topic headings, and we found 172 queries which clearly corresponded to some topic on the list; for instance, the topic *Christmas* was matched to the five queries "An Nollaig", "NOLLAIG", "Nollag", "nodlag", and "nodlaig". These 172 queries were matched to a total of 67 topics. We further restricted to those topics for which there were at least 100 transcribed stories in both Irish and English, leaving just 20 topics (*Riddles, Jokes, Fairy forts, The Great Famine, Entertainments and recreational activities, Folk medicine, Folk poetry, Food products, Religious tales, Clothing and accessories, Fianna, Feast of St Brigid, May, Halloween, Christmas, Prayers, Proverbs, Hardship, Graveyards, Potatoes*) and 72 of the original 172 queries. For each remaining topic, we randomly selected 100 Irish transcriptions and 100 English transcriptions from that topic in order to produce two test corpora of 2,000 documents each for our IR experiments. Finally, the English transcriptions were machine translated into Irish using the system described in Section 1.3 to allow us to evaluate the effectiveness of Irish language search queries for retrieving relevant English language documents.

The experiments differ only in the preprocessing that was applied to the documents in the test corpora before indexing and to the search queries before searching. The four experimental conditions are as follows:

- **Baseline**: For this experiment, all text was converted to lowercase, and Irish diacritics (á,é,í,ó,ú) are converted to ASCII (a,e,i,o,u). This setup is the default behavior of the existing *dúchas.ie* search engine as of May 2019.
- **Standardised**: For this experiment, the texts were standardised using the software described in Section 1.2, *An Caighdeánaitheoir*, and then lowercased and converted to ASCII as in the Baseline experiment.

- **Demutated**: Irish words are subject to so-called *initial mutations* which are triggered in certain semantic and syntactic environments and which cause the words to appear with different initial sounds. With rare exceptions, mutations in Irish can be detected and removed algorithmically in a trivial way because they are transparently reflected in the orthography (as is the case for Scottish Gaelic, but not for the other Celtic languages: Manx Gaelic, Welsh, Breton, and Cornish). For this experiment, the texts were standardised, lowercased, converted to ASCII, and finally all initial mutations were removed.
- **Lemmatised**: Irish nouns and adjectives are inflected according to their case and number, and verbs are inflected according to tense, mood, person, and number. For this experiment, the texts were standardised, lowercased, converted to ASCII, and finally lemmatised by means of a lemmatiser which is part of the open source Irish grammar checker *An Gramadóir*.[7] In the case of verbs, the lemmatised form is the singular imperative, which is the usual citation form in modern Irish dictionaries.

For each experimental setup and for both test corpora, we preprocess the 2,000 documents in the corpus and the 72 search engine queries in our final list according to one of the schemes above. We then perform a full text search on the corpus for each of the 72 queries, recording the total number of returned documents and the number of those deemed to be "relevant" (here, by definition, relevant documents are those labeled with the topic corresponding to the given search query). For example, consider the query "An Nollaig". This search is typical of many others in that it conforms to the standard orthography most familiar to users of the site, and as a consequence it returns no hits at all in the Baseline experiment because the texts in the test corpus where this phrase appears all use the prestandard spelling "An Nodlaig". On the other

---

[7] https://www.cadhan.com/gramadoir/

hand, in the Standardised experiment, the same query returns 21 documents from the test set, with 19 of the 21 carrying the correct label "Christmas". This yields a precision of 19/21 ≈ 0.90 and a recall of 0.19 (19 of the 100 relevant documents in the corpus) for this one query.

3 Results and discussion

In Table 1 we report Precision, Recall, and F-scores for each of the experiments described in the preceding section as applied to the corpus of Irish transcriptions, totalled over all 72 search queries. Table 2 provides the analogous results for the experiments applied to the corpus of machine-translated English transcriptions. Since the MT engine produces standard Irish as its output, we do not report results for the Standardised setup separately in Table 2 since those results are the same as for the Baseline.

Experiment	P	R	F
Baseline	0.67	0.10	0.17
Standardised	0.69	0.24	0.36
Demutated	0.70	0.29	0.41
Lemmatised	0.67	0.34	0.45

Table 1. Precision/recall results – Irish transcriptions.

Experiment	P	R	F
Translated + Baseline	0.59	0.15	0.24
" + Demutated	0.59	0.17	0.26
" + Lemmatised	0.60	0.21	0.31

Table 2. Precision/recall results – English transcriptions machine-translated to Irish.

Because the experimental setup is somewhat artificial, the absolute precision and recall values are not of great importance, but we do note in Table 1 a significant increase in recall over the baseline with the introduction of standardisation, and further increases with demutation and lemmatisation. These increases occur without any large decrease in precision.

In looking more closely at the results, a few things stand out. First, even with full standardisation and lemmatisation, a recall score of 0.34 seems low. This is due in part to the quality of some of the experimental search queries. For instance, a few of the 72 queries returned no results at all under any of the experiments. In one case, a search term was misspelled beyond the ability of the standardiser to correct it ("Oiche Shanmhna" for 'Halloween', correctly spelled "Oíche Shamhna" in the standard orthography). In another case, we generously interpreted the search query "ocras mór" (lit. 'great hunger') as an attempt to retrieve documents about the Irish potato famine, which indeed is sometimes referred to in English as "the Great Hunger", but for which the correct Irish is "(an) *Gorta* Mór" (lit. '(the) great famine'). Another class of low-recall queries appear to be searches for the topics themselves as opposed to searches for terms likely to appear in the full text transcriptions; e.g. the queries "filíocht" ('poetry'), "seanfhocail" ('proverbs'), "tomhaiseanna" ('riddles') all have very low recall values under all of the experimental conditions. This could be overcome by including the topic or other metadata in the search index.

The results in Table 2 show a similar increase in recall and no corresponding decrease in precision for the machine-translated English transcriptions. It is not surprising that the scores are somewhat lower than the ones in Table 1 since the machine translation engine is far from perfect and certainly introduces some noise into the process. On the other hand, the true baseline in this case is a recall of 0.0, since the current *dúchas.ie* search engine does not support retrieval of English transcriptions via Irish queries. We are therefore encouraged by these results, especially given that they were achieved through relatively straightforward use of existing language technologies.

4 Conclusion

We set out to improve full-text search results on *dúchas.ie* using language technology, building on crowdsourced transcriptions of folklore manuscripts. We have gathered together a set of existing language technologies to achieve this goal. These include tools to standardise, demutate, lemmatise, and translate the transcriptions of these folklore stories. We have shown that the introduction of these technologies can substantially improve search engine recall over a test set of actual user queries, with no appreciable drop in precision.

Motivated by these results, these technologies will be deployed in the search infrastructure on *dúchas.ie*. We envisage that standardisation and machine translation will be applied by default, as the query logs show that the website users tend to search using standard spellings. Demutation and lemmatisation will likely be optional, and raw searches will still be possible, however, exact implementation has yet to be specified. Search spelling suggestions using a standard lexicon and spelling distance algorithm could also be added.

A secondary outcome of this research was a list of common errors in the crowdsourced transcriptions. These terms were identified as errors by virtue of them not being present in a large corpus of texts from the period (Uí Dhonnchadha et al., 2014). We have categorised these errors, and they mostly involve (1) accented characters, (2) missing or spurious lenition (i.e. an orthographic 'h' following the initial consonant indicating phonetic weakening or deletion of the initial consonant (Welby et al., 2017)), or (3) the disordering of the letters 'iu' or 'iú'. This information will be used to improve instructions given to transcribers.

Lastly, other collections in the NFC being digitised by the Dúchas project include another large manuscript collection and a large audio collection. If these collections are made available for transcription by members of the public, and if such efforts are as successful as previous efforts, access to these collections could be improved using the language technologies tested in the paper.

Acknowledgements

The *Dúchas* project is funded by the Department of Culture, Heritage and the Gaeltacht with support from the National Lottery, University College Dublin, and the National Folklore Foundation, Ireland.

References

Arcan, Mihael, Caoilfhionn Lane, Eoin Ó Droighneáin, and Paul Buitelaar. 2016. IRIS: English-Irish Machine Translation System. *The International Conference on Language Resources and Evaluation*, Portorož, Slovenia.

Bhreathnach, Úna, Ciarán Mac Murchaidh, Gearóid Ó Cleircín, and Brian Ó Raghallaigh. 2019. Ní hualach do dhuine an léann: meithleacha pobail i ngort na Gaeilge. *Léachtaí Cholm Cille*, Maynooth, Ireland.

Dowling, Meghan, Teresa Lynn, Alberto Poncelas, and Andy Way. 2018. SMT versus NMT: Preliminary Comparisons for Irish. *Proceedings of the Workshop on Technologies for MT of Low Resource Languages*, Boston, MA, 12–20.

Dowling, Meghan, Teresa Lynn, Yvette Graham, and John Judge. 2016. English to Irish Machine Translation with Automatic Post-Editing. *2nd Celtic Language Technology Workshop*, Paris, France.

Dowling, Meghan, Lauren Cassidy, Eimear Maguire, Teresa Lynn, Ankit Srivastava, and John Judge. 2015. Tapadóir: Developing a statistical machine translation engine and associated resources for Irish. *4th LRL Workshop: Language Technologies in support of Less-Resourced Languages*, Poznan, Poland.

Galley, Michel, and Christopher D. Manning. 2008. A simple and effective hierarchical phrase reordering model. *Proceedings of the Conference on Empirical Methods in Natural Language Processing*. Association for Computational Linguistics, 848–856.

Heafield, Ken. 2011. KenLM: Faster and smaller language model queries. *Proceedings of the 6th Workshop on Statistical Machine Translation*. Association for Computational Linguistics, 187–197.

Irish Folklore Commission. 1937. *Irish Folklore and Tradition*. Department of Education, Dublin, Ireland.

Judge, John, Ailbhe Ní Chasaide, Rose Ní Dhubhda, Kevin P. Scannell, and Elaine Uí Dhonnchadha. 2012. The Irish Language in the Digital Age. *META-NET White Paper Series: Europe's Languages in the Digital Age.* Springer.

Ó Cathain, Séamas. 1988. Súil siar ar Scéim na Scol 1937-1938. *Sinsear*, 5:19–30.

Ó Cleircín, Gearóid, Anna Bale, and Brian Ó Raghallaigh. 2014. Dúchas.ie: ré nua i stair Chnuasach Bhéaloideas Éireann. *Béaloideas*, 82:85–99.

Ryan, Catherine. 2015. *MoTIF: Thesaurus Construction Guidelines*. Digital Repository of Ireland, Dublin, Ireland.

Scannell, Kevin. 2014. Statistical models for text normalization and machine translation. *Proceedings of the 1ˢᵗ Celtic Language Technology Workshop*, Dublin, Ireland, 33–40.

Uí Dhonnchadha, Elaine, Kevin Scannell, Ruairí Ó hUiginn, Eilís Ní Mhearraí, Máire Nic Mhaoláin, Brian Ó Raghallaigh, Gregory Toner, Séamus Mac Mathúna, Déirdre D'Auria, Eithne Ní Ghallchobhair, and Niall O'Leary. 2014. Corpas na Gaeilge (1882-1926): Integrating Historical and Modern Irish Texts. *Proceedings of the Workshop on Language Resources and Technologies for Processing and Linking Historical Documents and Archives – Deploying Linked Open Data in Cultural Heritage*, Reykjavik, Iceland, 12–18.

Welby, Pauline, Máire Ní Chiosáin, and Brian Ó Raghallaigh. 2017. Total eclipse of the heart? The production of eclipsis in two speaking styles of Irish. *Journal of the International Phonetic Association*, 47(2):125–153.

A Character-Level LSTM Network Model for Tokenizing the Old Irish text of the Würzburg Glosses on the Pauline Epistles

Adrian Doyle
National University of
Ireland Galway
`a.doyle35`
`@nuigalway.ie`

John P. McCrae
National University of
Ireland Galway
`john.mccrae`
`@insight-`
`centre.org`

Clodagh Downey
National University of
Ireland Galway
`clodagh.downey`
`@nuigalway.ie`

Abstract

This paper examines difficulties inherent in tokenization of Early Irish texts and demonstrates that a neural-network-based approach may provide a viable solution for historical texts which contain unconventional spacing and spelling anomalies. Guidelines for tokenizing Old Irish text are presented and the creation of a character-level LSTM network is detailed, its accuracy assessed, and efforts at optimising its performance are recorded. Based on the results of this research it is expected that a character-level LSTM model may provide a viable solution for tokenization of historical texts where the use of *Scriptio Continua*, or alternative spacing conventions, makes the automatic separation of tokens difficult.

1   Introduction

Dating from about the middle of the 8th century (Stifter, 2006), the Würzburg glosses on the Pauline epistles provide one of the earliest examples of Irish text contained in manuscript contemporary with the Old Irish period of "roughly the beginning of the 8th century to the middle of the 10th century A.D." (McCone, 1997, p. 163). Aside from the Würzburg collection, the later Milan and St. Gall glosses account for the only other large collections of Irish text in manuscripts from the period. As such, the contents of these glosses are of immense cultural significance, preserving some of the earliest dated writings in the language of the Irish people. All three sets of glosses have been collected in the two-volume *Thesaurus Palaeohibernicus* (Stokes and Strachan, 1901, 1903), where the relatively diplomatic editing of the text has retained orthographic features and information from the original manuscript content (Doyle, et al. 2018). Along with faithful reproduction of the text, however, come faithful reproductions of anomalies in word spacing and spelling. Section two of this paper will detail the difficulties associated with tokenizing the Würzburg glosses as they appear in *Thesaurus Palaeohibernicus* (TPH), and of tokenizing Old Irish text more generally. Section three will address the existence of comparable tokenization issues in modern languages, and research which has been carried out in order to provide solutions in these areas. Section four will provide a rationale for the creation of tokenization guidelines specifically for use with Old Irish text in a natural language processing (NLP) context, as well as discussing the results of an inter-annotator agreement experiment which has been carried out to assess these guidelines. Finally, section five will address the creation of a character-level, long short-term memory (LSTM) based recurrent neural network (RNN) model for tokenizing Old Irish, the effects of training the model on different standards of Old Irish text, and an evaluation of its performance at the task of tokenizing the Würzburg glosses.

2   Old Irish Orthography and Linguistic Considerations for Tokenization

The language encountered in Old Irish manuscripts is surprisingly uniform, with most

© 2019 The authors. This article is licensed under a Creative Commons 4.0 licence, no derivative works, attribution, CCBY-ND.

variation being diachronic, "the result of morphological development" (Thurneysen, 1946, p. 12). Despite this, the text is not as orthographically consistent as readers of Modern Irish will be accustomed to, and there are certain peculiarities to be observed. These peculiarities impact the potential to carry out even rudimentary pre-processing of text by conventional means for NLP purposes, and raise questions as to how different morphemes should be combined or separated to form tokens in the first place.

It is noted by Stifter that "the orthography of Irish changed over the course of time ... so that you may find in a manuscript one word written in Old Irish, the next in Modern Irish spelling and the third in a completely odd attempt at combining different standards" (2006, p.10). While this is more evident in later manuscripts, McCone has identified features more suggestive of Middle Irish than Old in manuscripts as early as that of the Würzburg glosses (1985), and there are linguistic differences evident between the three scribal hands of the Würzburg codex, with the text of the *prima manus* suggesting a more archaic form of Irish than that of the second and third hands (Stokes and Strachan, 1901; Thurneysen, 1946).

Additionally, the division of words in Old Irish manuscripts is not directly comparable to Modern Irish. Instead, word separation is based on linguistic stress patterns with spaces occurring between accentual units. In accordance with this spacing convention, "all words which are grouped round a single chief stress and have a close syntactic connexion with each other are written as one in the manuscripts" (Thurneysen, 1946, p. 24). As such it is common for conjunctions to fall together with a following verb (*articfea* = *ar ticfea*, "[it] will come"), for the article to fall together with a following noun (*indindocbál* = *ind indocbál*, "the glorification"), for the copula to fall together with a following predicate (*isdiasom* = *is dia-som*, "he is God"), as well as a variety of other combinations. There are also rarer instances where separate morphemes of what may be considered the same part of speech will be separated. Take, for example, the gloss, *.i. is inse nduit nitú nodnail acht ishé not ail* (Wb. 5b28), "i.e. it is impossible for you (sg.); it is not you (sg.) that nourishes it, but it is it that nourishes you (sg.)." In this example the verb, *ailid*, "to nourish", is used twice, in both cases combined with the empty prefix, *no*, used to infix a pronoun. While the infixed pronoun changes between the first usage, *nodnail*, "nourishes it", and the second, *not ail*, "nourishes you", the spacing introduced between the pronoun and the verbal root in the second instance is the more notable difference. What this example demonstrates is that, not only can spacing be lacking in Old Irish manuscripts where it would be desirable to inform tokenization at the boundaries of different parts of speech, but it can also be inserted within constituent parts of a verb. An automatic tokenizer capable of processing manuscript text will need, therefore, not only to introduce spacing where it does not already exist within the text, but also to remove it where it has been employed within one part of speech to separate two accentual units.

A final consideration, related to the previous example, should be given to the phenomenon of infixing pronouns within compound verbs in Old Irish. A variety of Old Irish verbs are formed by prefixing one or more preverbal particles to a following verbal root (Thurneysen, 1946; Stifter, 2006). The simple verb, *beirid*, "to carry", forms the root of the compound verbs, *dobeir*, "to give", and *asbeir*, "to say", for example. Thurneysen (1946) refers to the preverbal particles as prepositions, this being their historical origin, however, the prepositional function of these particles is often obscured by combination with the verbal root. In this sense Old Irish compound verbs might be compared to Modern English counterparts such as "oversee" and "withdraw", where the combination takes on a new sense of its own as a completely separate verb in meaning, whereby that meaning would be lost if the verbal root were to be split from the preposition element. In such cases the compound verb is typically considered to be a word in its own right, rather than the combination of its constituent parts, and hence, it requires its own token. This poses a minor problem as regards automatically tokenizing Irish compound verbs in that a tokenizer must not split these apart when encountered. A more challenging problem is presented, however, in the way Old Irish deals with pronouns which form the objects of these compound verbs. These are infixed between the preverbal particle and the verbal root, effectively splitting what might ideally be considered a single token and requiring that another token be placed within it. To exemplify this issue, where the verb mentioned above, *dobeir*, "he gives", appears with the first singular infixed pronoun, *-m*, it becomes *dombeir*, "he gives me".

Webster and Kit (1992) make the point that the "simplicity of recognising words in English [results] from the existence of space marks as explicit delimiters". It is, perhaps based on this same notion that Hông Phuong et al. (2008) claim "a tokenizer which simply replaces blanks with word boundaries ... is already quite accurate" for alphabetic scripts. Unfortunately, for the reasons outlined above, such an approach is not necessarily feasible with Old Irish texts. Before tokenization can be carried out decisions must be made regarding the treatment of issues outlined in this paper. These decisions will necessarily depend on the ultimate goal of the NLP tasks for which tokenization is to take place. It will, in any case, be necessary to decide whether to separate parts of speech which have been combined into accentual units, or to leave the manuscript spacing stand. It will also be important to consider how compound verbs, especially those bearing infixed pronouns, should be tokenized. The treatment of such issues, for the purposes of this paper, will be discussed further in section four.

3   A Review of Tokenization Solutions for Comparable Languages.

While the combination of issues outlined above, which hinder automatic tokenization prospects for Old Irish texts, are uncommon, particularly in European languages utilising the Roman alphabet, they are not all necessarily unique. Latin itself was typically written in *scriptio continua*, a writing style devoid of any spacing or marking to indicate word separation, until about the seventh century when Irish scribes introduced practice of word spacing to the European continent (Saenger, 1997). This timeframe would suggest that the Würzburg glosses, dating from about the middle of the eighth century, are quite an early example of text which demonstrates such spacing. The practice would not become the standard in European texts until about the thirteenth century. Tolmachev et al. (2018) present a toolkit for developing morphological analysers for *scriptio continua* languages, which utilises RNN and linear neural net models.

Turning towards modern natural languages further comparisons can be made. Tokenization solutions which have been developed for languages including Finnish (Haverinen et al., 2013; Lankinen et al., 2016), Arabic (Habash and Rambow, 2005) and Vietnamese (Hông Phuong et al., 2008) may provide a basis for developing an Old Irish tokenizer. In the case of Vietnamese, Hông Phuong et al. explain that the language uses an alphabetic script, but that spacing is used not only to separate words, but also the syllables which make up words. Furthermore, syllables,

taken in isolation, are typically words themselves. When combined with other syllables, words of complex meaning are created. As such, the problem faced by Vietnamese in terms of word segmentation is comparable to that of Old Irish where compound verbs are formed by combining two or more commonly occurring parts of speech. The solution presented by Hông Phuong et al. combines a technique using finite-state automata, regular expression parsing, and a matching strategy which is augmented by statistical methods to resolve segmentation ambiguities. While these linguistic ambiguities are more comparable to the case of Old Irish, the solution requires the creation of rule-based finite-state automata, which is unfeasible in the case of Old Irish, where morphological complexity, spelling irregularities, and relative scarcity of text would suggest that manually morphologically analysing the text may be a more time efficient approach. By contrast, the approach adopted for Finnish by Lankinen et al. (2016) may provide a more viable solution for tokenizing Old Irish text. This approach utilises an LSTM based language model which uses characters as input and output, but which still processes word level embeddings.

3.1   Potential for Adapting Solutions to Old Irish Text

Conventional knowledge would suggest that, where limited text resources exist, a rule-based approach is likely to produce more accurate results than statistical or neural alternatives, albeit, often requiring more human effort. While this largely holds for languages with relatively simple morphology, like modern English, the comparatively complex morphology of Old Irish may make such an approach more difficult. Uí Dhonnchadha (2009) has produced a rule based morphological analyser for modern Irish using finite-state transducers, however, Fransen suggests in a forthcoming publication that a comparable approach may pose more difficulty for Old Irish where "Unpredictable inflectional patterns resulting from irregular syncope and analogy in inflectional patterns challenge a linguistically motivated, rule-based derivational approach." This extra complexity is compounded, Fransen continues, by a lack of resources necessary for the task, for example, "the absence of an exhaustive list of Old Irish verbs and information about stem type and stem formation." The human effort required to create such resources, and to encode rules to account for most textual eventualities, must be weighed against the effort required for a human to manually carry out a given task on the reasonably sized, but limited, extant corpus of Old Irish literature. Given these particular circumstances, an argument may be made for the application of neural approaches to aid philologists in such tasks, even if it is unreasonable to expect particularly high accuracy without a large corpus on which to train.

As some repositories of machine-readable Old Irish text are available online a character-level LSTM based RNN approach may provide a more feasible solution than a purely rule-based model for Old Irish tokenization. The Milan and St. Gall glosses are available in online databases (Griffith, 2013; Bauer et al., 2017), meanwhile the 3,511 Würzburg glosses which appear in TPH are available in digital text (Doyle, 2018). The Corpus of Electronic Texts (CELT) (Färber, 1997) contains a collection of digital texts in Irish from the Old, Middle and Early Modern periods, and POMIC (Lash, 2014) contains a small collection of parsed Old and Middle Irish texts. As the large majority of word spacing used in the text of the Würzburg glosses does occur at word boundaries it may be possible to train a language model on these glosses themselves, and thereafter to use this model to recognise word boundaries in Old Irish text. Hence, it may be possible to tokenize the glosses using a model based on those same, untokenized glosses. As many word forms, particularly those which are always unstressed, almost never occur in the glosses without forming part of an accentual unit, however, the ability of such a model may be limited, and only common word boundary types may be recognisable. Another option is to train the model on texts drawn from the CELT collection. As many of these texts have been rigorously edited by scholars, both before and after being digitised, they not only provide a large source of text on which to train a language model, but a source of text in which word spacing is highly normalised and not based on accentual units. Normalisation standards vary from one editor to another, however, and the content of prose texts on CELT may not accurately reflect the religious vocabulary of the glosses. For these reasons, a set of guidelines for tokenizing Old Irish text have been created, and these will be discussed in section four. These guidelines will provide a standard against which to assess the accuracy of tokenizers built using LSTM RNN based language models which have been trained on text from the Würzburg glosses and from CELT.

4   Guidelines for Tokenizing Old Irish

Without consistent word spelling and consistent spacing at word boundaries tokenization by the conventional means of dividing a text into tokens based on spacing is not plausible. It has been shown in section two that the spacing conventions typically employed in Old Irish text do not permit such conventional tokenization into separate parts of speech. While, for some NLP tasks, it may be preferable to allow manuscript spacing conventions to stand and, thereby, compile a lexicon of accentual units which occur in a text, for many downstream NLP tasks it will be preferable to split such units into their component words. Fransen's (forthcoming) work, for example, outlines that "Morphological parsing operates on the word level, and words are defined as strings surrounded by space", hence, for this task it is a necessary prerequisite for words to be bounded by spaces. This necessity requires, if not a clear definition of what a word is considered to be in a given language, then, at least, a vague general notion of which combinations of morphemes constitute a word, and which constitute lower-level parts of speech. While this paper makes no attempt to provide such a definition, it has been necessary to develop a set of guidelines for tokenization, and these will be outlined in this section.

4.1   Extant Editorial Standards for Old Irish

In a language generally written without regard to rigid word boundaries, and instead divided at stress boundaries, the notion of a word is somewhat elusive. This factor contributes, no doubt, to the variation in standards for editing Old Irish texts, mentioned in section three. To exemplify this issue, take the commonly combined morphemes, *inso*, "this", frequently appearing in Irish manuscripts both within texts themselves and in many titles. In many editorial standards for Old Irish, these would be split apart into the article, *in*, and the demonstrative pronoun, *so*. Despite this, Stifter's practice in *Sengoídelc* (2006) is to represent the combination separated with a hyphen, *in-so*, both in a section explaining the use of demonstratives (p. 103) and in continued examples thereafter (p. 130, 26.3, eg. 6). It may not have been intended to suggest that the combination be treated as a single token, however, it nicely demonstrates the variation which can exist, even in standardised Old Irish texts.

Another area where much variation occurs in edited texts is in the treatment of enclitics, such as the emphatic suffixes and the anaphoric *suide*. In many editions the decision to present such morphemes as either enclitic, attached to a preceding part of speech by a hyphen, or as tokens separated from a preceding word, is dependent on which of the two is stressed. One edition of *Tochmarc Emire la Coinculaind* available on CELT (Färber, 1997), for example, contains the line, "*Atbert som fris-som...*", "he said to him". While significant linguistic reasons may exist for editorial decisions to treat comparable parts of speech in varying ways, this variety does not provide a good basis for tokenization. If, as suggested earlier, the goal is to split parts of speech without regard to accentual units, all occurrences of individual parts of speech which are performing an identical function should ideally be tokenized consistently. In other texts on the site preverbal particles are variously hyphenated, completely attached, or separated from the following verb by a space. In the case of particles like *ro* and *no*, the practice of separating them from the following verb may in some cases be desirable in order to identify very low level parts of speech at a later stage, however, this can create difficulty when preverbs are compounded and reduced as with *ro* in *do·á-r-bas*, "has been shown" (Thurneysen, 1946, p. 340). The problem in these cases is that the reduced particle is not typically removed or separated from the verbal root in editions. Again, this creates a situation where a part of speech with a single function is treated differently when it does not occur immediately at the beginning of a verb. Ideally a more universal editorial standard might be adhered to, however, in lieu of such a standard, the guidelines proposed below for tokenization will be based largely on extant editorial standards and will specify the reason for any variation from such standards.

4.2 Tokenization Guidelines for this Experiment

In developing guidelines for tokenization Old Irish, a balance must be struck between tailoring tokens to account for the complex morphology of the language and tailoring them to account for the relative scarcity of text resources which are digitally available. The lack of a large, universally standardised, corpus of Old Irish text limits the amount of data with which to train statistical or neural network models. As such, the guidelines for tokenization listed below have been developed so as to avoid creating a wide variety of infrequently occurring tokens. As such, frequently occurring affixes such as demonstrative and emphatic suffixes are always separated from preceding tokens and considered to be tokens themselves. An exception to this rule is made for preverbal particles, which are instead taken to be a constituent part of a following verb. While this will create a larger variety of verbal tokens, it has been shown above that the separation of these particles is not always feasible, particularly where they are compounded or reduced.

The case of verbs containing infixed pronouns requires particular attention. These guidelines recommend treating the entire verbal complex as an individual token. This will allow for verbs with infixed pronouns to be treated as morphological variants of the base verb form in part-of-speech tagging, which is necessary as the inclusion of an infixed pronoun can affect the morphology of the preverbal particle in some instances. Thurneysen points out that "the *-o* of *ro, no, do, fo* is lost before initial *a*" (1946, p. 257). For example, *dogníu*, "I do", loses the *-o* of the preverbal particle, *do*, and becomes *dagníu*, "I do it", with the third person, singular, neuter pronoun, *a*, infixed. This morphological change to the particle constitutes an alteration of the verb, and therefore would require the entry of an alternative form in a lexicon. However, as this form cannot occur without the infixed pronoun which is causing it, the entire complex should be taken as being the alternate form. Future work will look at part-of-speech tagging, and the possibility of extracting infixed pronouns and tagging them separately at that stage will be explored. In the current work, however, they will be treated, as outlined above, as internalised tokens.

Aside from internalised tokens, the guidelines account for one more form of specialised token. Where forms of a significant part of speech such as the article, the copula, or possessive pronouns occur in reduced or altered form when combined with other tokens, these forms are considered to be conjoined tokens. For example, where the article is preceded by prepositions such as *co, i* and *fri*, giving rise to combined forms such as *cosin, isnaib* and *frisna*, the separated forms of the article, *-sin, -snaib,* and *-sna* are conjoined tokens. Similarly, when possessive pronouns precede or follow vowels, they take on a conjoined form, with examples such as *id*, "in your" and *manam* (Wb. 17c4a), "my soul", containing the conjoined tokens *-d* and *m-* respectively. While conjoined tokens in the guidelines are displayed with a hyphen to demonstrate their dependency on a preceding or following token, this is removed in implementation, hence, *manam* should be rendered *m anam*.

Aside from the token types outlined in this section and those parts of speech mentioned earlier in this paper, there are few common disagreements in editorial standards. It is hoped that the guidelines outlined here will provide a reasonable baseline for measuring success in automatic tokenization, however, on the basis of varying requirements for varying tasks, a different style of tokenization may be required, and so, alteration to these guidelines.

4.3   Inter-Annotator Agreement

An inter-annotator agreement experiment has been carried out using the tokenization guidelines detailed above. Four annotators have been shown forty-one glosses selected from the Würzburg corpus (Doyle, 2018), and asked to introduce or remove spacing as necessary in accordance with the guidelines. Annotators were instructed not to introduce or remove any letters, hyphens or other non-space characters. During the timeframe of the experiment three annotators were PhD candidates in the field of Early Irish, and the fourth was a postdoctoral researcher in the same field.

Before being shown the guidelines, two of the annotators were asked to perform the task of separating words, by introducing or removing spaces only, based on their intuitive understanding of how word division should be implemented. These two annotators were shown the guidelines only after this first run had been completed, and were asked again to carry out the task, this time adhering to the guidelines. This allows a comparison to be made between annotators working both with and without the guidelines.

.i. biuusa oc irbáig dar far cennsi fri maccidóndu
.i. biuu sa oc irbáig dar far cenn si fri maccidóndu

Figure 1: Agreement (green) and disagreement (red) between two annotators

Agreement between annotators was measured by determining which particular letters in a string are followed by a space in any annotator's work, then comparing two annotators work to see if they agreed on the inclusion or exclusion of a space at a given point, or if they disagreed with one including a space, and another not doing so. See

an example of agreement and disagreement between two annotators in Figure 1.

	Cohen's Kappa Score
Pair 1 – (A1 + A2)	0.469
Pair 2 – (A1 + A3)	0.349
Pair 3 – (A1 + A4)	0.655
Pair 4 – (A2 + A3)	0.191
Pair 5 – (A2 + A4)	0.457
Pair 6 – (A3 + A4)	0.297
Annotator Average Score	0.403
No Guidelines	-0.058

Table 1: Inter-annotator agreement Cohen's kappa scores for each pair of annotators, and average

Cohen's kappa coefficient was used to compare the work of each pair of annotators using the guidelines. Table 1 shows that the highest agreement between two annotators using the guidelines was substantial at 0.65, while the lowest, at 0.19, was higher than would be expected by chance. The average score between pairs of annotators was 0.40 suggesting that the guidelines may require further clarification on some points. It is, however, noteworthy that the guidelines seem to ensure higher agreement than might be expected of annotators working without them, at least, when compared to the score of the two annotators work before they had been shown the guidelines, -0.058.

The results of this inter-annotator experiment will be used in section five as a means of comparing human performance at a tokenization task against that of the LSTM-based tokenizer model detailed in this paper.

5   A Character-Level LSTM Recurrent Neural Network Model for Tokenizing Old Irish

A Character-Level LSTM RNN model was created using TensorFlow and Keras. The purpose of the RNN is to model the language of the text it is trained on and develop an understanding of which sequences of characters are likely to indicate a word ending. A function has been developed so that this model can be utilised to identify points in a text where it is likely that word division should be added, and spacing is introduced at these points, thereby, allowing tokenization to be carried out by more conventional means. The development of this tokenizer and its evaluation is detailed in this section.

5.1 Pre-processing Text for Training and Evaluation

It was determined that the text of the Würzburg glosses (Doyle, 2018) contained fifty-two characters once all Latin text, and all editorial punctuation, commentary and brackets had been removed. An arbitrary, out of vocabulary character was introduced for use in padding sequences, bringing the character count to fifty-three. The only remaining punctuation in the glosses occurs in abbreviations such as *.i.* and *t.* In these instances, the punctuation which occurs is taken to be part of the token, hence, such punctuation was not removed in pre-processing. It is also noteworthy that, with the exception of some roman numerals and Latin names, all of which had been removed by this point in the processing, very few upper-case letters are used throughout the glosses.

The forty-one glosses utilised in the inter-annotator agreement experiment were removed from the corpus to be used as a test set in a later evaluation stage. At this point the remaining glosses were concatenated to form a single string. This string was the first of two training sets used in this experiment. The second training set was drawn from texts available on CELT (Färber, 1997). Ten texts were selected which were deemed both to be reasonably long and also to be edited to a standard comparable to one another:

- Táin Bó Regamna
- Táin Bó Fraích
- Táin Bó Cúailnge Recension I
- Táin Bó Cúalnge from the Book of Leinster
- Compert Con Chulainn
- Serglige Con Culainn
- Tochmarc Emire la Coinculaind (Harl. 5280)
- Tochmarc Emire la Coinculaind (Rawlinson B 512)
- Fled Bricrend (Codex Vossianus)
- The Training of Cúchulainn

The texts were concatenated together to form one string, and all characters were changed to lower-case. A number of characters which did not transfer cleanly into UTF-8 format had to be manually corrected. Other alterations included the automatic removal of editorial notes and folio information, editions which use the letter *v*, which does not occur in the Würzburg character-set, were altered and the letter *u* was substituted in its place. Finally, in an attempt to align the various editorial standards with the tokenization guidelines, a script was written using regular expressions to identify common preverbal particles which had been separated from a following verb and attach them to it, and similarly, to find common suffixes attached to preceding words by hyphenation and detach them. This approach runs the risk of accidentally splitting genuine tokens where part of the token matches the regular expression used. It would be preferable to train on a corpus where the editor had deliberately edited using this standard, however, this was the most feasible solution with the available editions. With the two separate training corpora having been created, the following steps were applied to each before training on them.

The training corpora were sequenced into strings of ten. For every string of eleven characters in the training corpus, the first ten characters were added to a list of training strings, and the eleventh was added to a set of associated labels. Each label, therefore, is the character which directly follows the preceding string of ten characters. Finally, each sequence of characters, and label, were converted into one-hot vectors with a length of fifty-three to account for each character. Before training, ten percent of sequences and labels were set aside. During the training process these were used to validate the accuracy of the model by testing it on unseen sequences. This step helped to prevent overfitting of the model.

5.2 Developing the Model

It was decided to build a character level model so that the network could learn which sequences of characters are most likely to signify a word ending. LSTM cells were utilised in the RNN to enable dependencies to be learned by the model over long distances, as some rare morphological features may occur infrequently in a text, and hence, may be spread far apart in a string of characters. Backpropagation is used by RNNs in order to improve at a given task over time. Error signals flow backwards through the network and weights between cells are recalibrated to improve accuracy. Over time conventional networks' evaluation of backpropagated error signals tend to either increase or decrease exponentially (Hochreiter and Schmidhuber, 1997). This results in a network which may be accurate in the short term, but which becomes increasingly incapable of pattern recognition in the long term, for example, over long strings of text. LSTM RNNs attempt to overcome this issue, whereby error evaluation either explodes or vanishes over time, by intelligently "forgetting" error information as it becomes irrelevant to the system. This is an important improvement as, generally, the more data which a network can train on, the more accurately the network can identify patterns. Sundermeyer et al. write of language modelling, "the probability distribution over word sequences can be directly learned from large amounts of text data..." (2015, p. 517). A similar approach will be used here, instead attempting to learn probability distributions over character sequences in order to identify word endings.

No. of Hidden Layers	2
Hidden Layer Size	53
Input Format	53x10 Vector
Output Format	53 (Model 1) **OR** 2 (Model 2)
Optimiser	Adam
Loss Function	Categorical Cross-entropy

Table 2: Hyperparameters for the RNN

Through experimentation it was determined that the most accurate model was achieved utilising two hidden layers of LSTM cells. The number of cells in each hidden layer was equal to the length of the one-hot vectors, as this was found to be the most accurate without causing overfitting. No attempt was made to train using batches. See table 2 for more information on the model's hyperparameters.

Two variants of the model were created. The first was designed to guess the following character based on the sequence of ten characters it was shown, and the second was designed only to guess only whether the following character would be a space or not. These will be referred to as Model 1, and Model 2, respectively.

5.3 Designing the Tokenizer

At first, a function was created in order to tokenize strings of text using the model. The function takes each character in the string and uses the model to determine if the next character should be a space or not. The next subsection will detail how the models and tokenizers were evaluated, however, this tokenizer's performance was deemed to be unsatisfactory.

To improve performance a second, reverse model was trained. This model works backwards through the training text and attempts to predict a character preceding a given input sequence. Once this model had been trained the tokenization function was adapted to include it. For each character in a string which is fed into the function, the forward model predicts whether a space should be introduced after it. If the forward model predicts a space, the reverse model is shown the following ten characters to make a prediction whether a space should precede them. A space is introduced only if the two models agree that a space should be introduced at a given point. Similarly, the function looks at spaces already in the string which is fed into it and seeks agreement from the models as to whether to remove the space or leave it in the string. Finally, the function outputs the string with new spaces included, and potentially with some spaces removed. This combined forward-reverse tokenizer was found to be more accurate than one based on either the forward or reverse models alone.

5.4 Evaluation

During the training of models, a wide variety of parameters were experimented with in order to produce the best possible model. At this stage training accuracy was measured using TensorFlow's built in TensorBoard. This also enabled loss to be measured over the time taken to train a given model.

As mentioned above, ten percent of all training sequences were split off and used to validate accuracy and loss scores by periodically testing the model-in-training on unseen sequences and labels. At the point in training when validation loss began to increase, training was stopped in order to prevent overfitting. This generally occurred at about 24 epochs when training on sequences from the first training set drawn from the glosses, and at about 8 epochs when training on the larger collection of texts of the second training set. It is also notable that the accuracy for Model 1 was consistently lower than that of Model 2. The highest validation accuracy score for Model 1 peaked at about 36%, while that of Model 2 reached a peak of 92% accuracy. These scores were not apparently affected by the training set used, and both training sets used with Model 1 reached the 92% accuracy score on the validation set. This suggests that the task of predicting word endings only was easier for models than the task of predicting any of the potential fifty-two characters.

While an accuracy of 92% is reasonably high for an RNN trained on a limited amount of text, it should be remembered that a tokenizer built on a model with this accuracy score would insert or remove a space incorrectly about once for every ten characters in a given string. This may explain why the performance of the forward only tokenizer design was unsatisfactory. In any case, the accuracy score of a model is not necessarily an accurate indicator of how well a tokenizer built on that model will work. This is especially true in the case of tokenizers built on Model 1, where the tokenizer function ignores all character predictions other than ones which would introduce or remove a space.

Tokenization accuracy, therefore, needs to be measured by separate means to those described above for evaluating LSTM models. For this purpose, four tokenizers were used to tokenize the forty-one glosses used in the inter-annotator agreement assessment. Information regarding the model and training set used to create each tokenizer can be seen in table 3.

Tokenizer	Model	Training Set
T1	Model 1	Wb. text
T2	Model 1	CELT texts
T3	Model 2	Wb. text
T4	Model 2	CELT texts

Table 3: Tokenizers, models and training texts

In order to quantify the success of each tokenizer the output of each model was compared against the work of each annotator, again using Cohen's kappa coefficient (see table 4).

	A1	A2	A3	A4
T1	0.2703	0.2225	0.2842	0.2693
T2	0.0297	0.0172	0.0563	0.0355
T3	0.2494	0.1974	0.2613	0.2431
T4	0.1836	0.1408	0.1805	0.1701

Table 4: Measurement of annotators' work (A1-4) compared against output of tokenizer models (T1-4) using Cohen's kappa

These results show that no tokenizer performed worse than the two human annotators working without guidelines, while the better performing tokenizers show a higher score than at least one pairing of human annotators working with guidelines. This seems to suggest that a neural approach may provide a feasible solution for automatic word segmentation in unedited Old Irish texts. It is interesting that the best performing tokenizer (T1) was trained on the glosses themselves, rather than on a larger amount of text which has been edited to a desirable standard. It may be the case that out-of-vocabulary terminology in the glosses reduces the effectiveness of models trained on prose text. Future work, therefore, will focus on applying a bootstrapping approach to tokenization of the glosses. Models will be periodically trained on manually tokenized glosses and tested against this same test set until an improvement is noted over the current models. It is expected also that training on a corpus of edited gloss material will increase performance, therefore, going forward, attempts will be made to improve the techniques detailed here by training similar tokenizers on the text of the St. Gall glosses (Bauer, et al., 2017). Further improvements may be gleaned by the addition of a simple rule-based output layer which would make sure that easily identifiable features, such as common particles, abbreviations, and initial mutations, are appropriately bounded by spacing.

6   Conclusion

This paper has examined difficulties inherent in tokenization of Early Irish texts and presented guidelines for tokenization developed with these particular difficulties in mind. These guidelines have been shown to improve inter-annotator agreement on a word segmentation task. A character-level LSTM based RNN was developed to automatically tokenize Old Irish text and demonstrated potential. It may be possible to improve upon performance by training on a corpus of pre-processed glosses, as prose material appears to be less suitable, and by the addition of a rule-based output layer.

Acknowledgements

Particular thanks are owed to the following annotators who have, thus far, contributed their time and expertise to the inter-annotator agreement experiment detailed in this paper: Maria Hallinan (NUIG), Dr. Daniel Watson (DIAS), Theodorus Fransen (TCD), and Jody Buckley-Coogan (QUB).
This work has been funded by the National University of Ireland, Galway, through the Digital Arts and Humanities Programme, and is also supported by the Irish Research Council through the Government of Ireland Postgraduate Scholarship Programme.
Dr. McCrae's research is supported in part by a research grant from Science Foundation Ireland (SFI) under Grant Number SFI/12/RC/2289, co-funded by the European Regional Development Fund, and the European Union's Horizon 2020 research and innovation programme under grant agreement No 731015, ELEXIS - European Lexical Infrastructure and grant agreement No 825182, Prêt-à-LLOD.

References

Bauer, Bernhard, Rijcklof Hofman and Pádraic Moran. 2017. *St. Gall Priscian Glosses, version 2.0* <www.stgallpriscian.ie/> (Accessed: 08/05/2019).

Doyle, Adrian. 2018. Würzburg Irish Glosses, <www.wuerzburg.ie> (Accessed: 08/05/2019)

Doyle, Adrian, John P. McCrae and Clodagh Downey. 2018. *Preservation of Original Orthography in the Construction of an Old Irish Corpus*. Proceedings of the 3rd Workshop on Collaboration and Computing for Under-Resourced Languages (CCURL 2018). Miyazaki, Japan.

Färber, Beatrix (ed.). 1997. *CELT Corpus of Electronic Texts*. <https://celt.ucc.ie/irlpage.html> (Accessed: 08/05/2019)

Fransen, Theodorus. Forthcoming. *Automatic Morphological Analysis and Interlinking of Historical Irish Cognate Verb Forms*. Elliott Lash, Fangzhe Qiu and David Stifter (eds.). Corpus-based Approaches to Morphosyntactic Variation and Change in Medieval Celtic Languages. De Gruyter, Berlin.

Griffith, Aaron. 2013. *A Dictionary of the Old-Irish Glosses*. <https://www.univie.ac.at/indogermanistik/milan_g lgloss/> (Accessed: 08/05/2019).

Haverinen, Katri, Jenna Nyblom, Timo Viljanen, Veronika Laippala, Samuel Kohonen, Anna Missilä, Stina Ojala, Tapio Salakoski and Filip Ginter. 2013. *Building the essential resources for Finnish: the Turku Dependency Treebank*. Language Resources and Evaluation.

Habash, Nizar and Owen Rambow. 2005. *Arabic Tokenization, Part-of-Speech Tagging and Morphological Disambiguation in One Fell Swoop*. Proceedings of the 43rd Annual Meeting of the ACL, pp. 573-580.

Hochreiter, Sepp and Jürgen Schmidhuber. 1997. *Long Short-Term Memory*. Neural Computation, Vol. 9, No. 8, pp. 1735-1780.

Hông Phuong, Lê, Nguyên Thi Minh Huyên, Azim Roussanaly and Hô Tuòng Vinh. 2008. *A Hybrid Approach to Word Segmentation of Vietnamese Texts*. 2nd International Conference on Language and Automata Theory and Applications, Tarragona, Spain.

Kavanagh, Séamus and Dagmar S. Wodtko. 2001. *A Lexicon of the Old Irish Glosses in the Würzburg Manuscript of the Epistles of St. Paul*. Verlag der Österreichischen Akademie der Wissenschaften, Vienna.

Lankinen, Matti, Hannes Heikinheimo, Pyry Takala, Tapani Raiko and Juha Karhunen. 2016. *A Character-Word Compositional Neural Language Model for Finnish.*

Lash, Elliott. 2014. *The Parsed Old and Middle Irish Corpus (POMIC)*. Version 0.1. <https://www.dias.ie/celt/celt-publications-2/celt-the-parsed-old-and-middle-irish-corpus-pomic/> (Accessed: 08/05/2019).

Lynn, Teresa. 2012. *Medieval Irish and Computational Linguistics*. Australian Celtic Journal, 10:13-28.

McCone, Kim. 1985. *The Würzburg and Milan Glosses: Our Earliest Sources of 'Middle Irish'*. Ériu, 36:85-106.

McCone, Kim. 1997. *The Early Irish Verb*. An Sagart, Maynooth, 2nd edition.

Mullen, Lincoln. A., Kenneth Benoit, Os Keyes, Dmitry Selivanov and Jeffrey Arnold. 2018. *Fast, Consistent Tokenization of Natural Language Text*. Journal of Open Source Software.

Saenger, Paul. 1997. *Space Between Words: the Origins of Silent Reading*, Stanford University Press, Stanford, California

Stifter, David. 2006. *Sengoidelc*. Syracuse University Press, New York.

Stokes, Whitley and John Strachan. (Eds.). 1901. *Thesaurus Palaeohibernicus Volume I*. The Dublin Institute for Advanced Studies, Dublin, 3rd edition.

Stokes, Whitley and John Strachan. (Eds.). 1903. *Thesaurus Palaeohibernicus Volume II*. The Dublin Institute for Advanced Studies, Dublin, 3rd edition.

Sundermeyer, Martin, Hermann Ney and Ralf Schlüter. 2015. *From Feedforward to Recurrent LSTM Neural Networks for Language Modeling*. Audio Speech and Language Processing IEEE/ACM Transactions on, Vol. 23, No. 3, pp. 517-529.

Thurneysen, Rudolf. 1946. *A Grammar of Old Irish*. The Dublin Institute for Advanced Studies, Dublin.

Tolmachev, Arseny, Daisuke Kawahara and Sadao Kurohashi. 2018. Juman++: *A Morphological Analysis Toolkit for Scriptio Continua*. ACL.

Uí Dhonnchadha, Elaine. 2009. *Part-of-Speech Tagging and Partial Parsing for Irish Using Finite-State Transducers and Constraint Grammar*. PhD Thesis, Dublin City University.

Webster, Jonathan J. and Chunyu Kit. 1992. *Tokenization as the Initial Phase in NLP*. Proceedings of the 14th Conference on Computational Linguistics, Nantes, France.

A Green Approach for an Irish App (Refactor, reuse and keeping it real)

Monica Ward
Dublin City University
Ireland
monica.ward@dcu.ie

Maxim Mozgovoy
University of Aizu
Japan
mozgovoy@u-aizu.ac.jp

Marina Purgina
University of Aizu
Japan
mapurgina@gmail.com

Abstract

There is a lack of apps for learning Irish, and while there is a potential demand for such apps, good quality, pedagogically sound apps are difficult to develop. This paper reports on a green approach to develop an app for learning Irish. It refactors and reuses an existing app (WordBricks, Mozgovoy and Effimov, 2013) and adapts it for Irish. The app uses existing Irish NLP resources, specifically Uí Dhonnchadha's Finiate Stage Mophological Analyser (2002) and Lynn's Irish parser and treebank (2016), as part of the app. The app was developed in conjunction with teachers to ensure that it was curriculum-aligned and testing with the target learner group (primary school learners) before actual deployment in a real classroom. The app has been used by a variety of classes, ranging in age from 7 to 11 years of age. Results indicate that the app is usable and enjoyable for learners and teachers report that it is beneficial for their students. It would not have been possible to build the app in a relatively short period of time without adopting a green (i.e. refactor, reuse and real) paradigm.

1 Introduction

Irish is one of the two official languages of Irish along with English. However, only a relatively small percentage of the population speak it as an L1. Nearly all students study the language in school with primary school children studying the language for around 30 minutes each day and secondary school students for 160 minutes a week. The teaching of the language is currently very traditional, with a 'chalk and talk' and 'sage on the stage' approach prevailing. There is a space for more modern resources for the teaching and learning or Irish. This paper provides an overview of a mobile Irish language app, Irish WordBricks, that allows learners to practice the construction of grammatically correct sentences in Irish. The Irish WordBricks app uses a visual learning paradigm and can be used by learners of all ages.

1.1 Language Learning Apps

Language learning is difficult and anything that helps the learning process is to be welcomed. Motivation is very important in learning (Dörnyei & Ushioda, 2013; Ushioda, 2013), particularly in language learning as the challenges involved and the application of the knowledge acquired may be difficult. In recent years, there has been an increasing use of technology in the language learning process. One area of expanding interest is that of language learning apps. These apps let students learn a language on a mobile device, with an anytime, anywhere approach. Some of the most commonly used apps are Duolingo, Buso and Memrise. These apps are free to use for the basic components and learners can pay extra to have access to more advanced features and additional resources. Many of these apps are used in the informal learning space, but could be used in the formal as well. Duolingo (n.d.) is probably the best know language learning app and is currently available in 33 languages, mainly the most commonly spoken languages but it also includes Irish (954,000 learners), Welsh (347, 000 learners), Navajo (251,000 learners) and Klingon (500,000 learners). It works on a translation approach whereby learners have to translate works between their L1 and the target L2 in both directions. It uses a gamified approach to learning (Nacke and Deterding, 2017; Reinhardt, J., & Sykes, 2014) and it can be beneficial for some learners. Duolingo uses a community

© 2019 The authors. This article is licensed under a Creative Commons 4.0 licence, no derivative works, attribution, CCBY-ND.

development approach but also has a team of developers working behind the scenes.

1.2 Irish App Development Challenges

Language learning apps, such as Duolingo, Buso and Memrise, are often enjoyable and can be pedagogically informed. However, they may not be suitable in some learning contexts. For example, they may not cover all aspects of the language learning process (which is very difficult to do), their pedagogical approach may focus on one particular strategy and learners may have needs that are not met by these apps. Learners cannot construct their own sentences and are constrained by the sentences already predefined in the app. It would be beneficial to have other apps and technology-based resources for learners.

There are many challenges to be overcome to develop a language learning app for any language. The field of Computer Assisted Language Learning (CALL) (Beaty, 2013; Levy and Stockwell, 2013) is a multi-disciplinary one involving language teachers, linguistics, pedagogical specialists, Natural Language Processing (NLP) experts, software engineers, programmers, user interface designers and, of course, language learners. Access to sufficient financial resources, adequate time and availability of relevant experts is also important. This is the ideal scenario and one that rarely exist, even for some of the Most Commonly Taught Languages (MCTLs). In reality, CALL researchers and practitioners must be resourceful and use whatever resources and skills are available to them. The challenges are even greater for Less Commonly Taught Languages (LCTLs) where there is usually less of everything. There is usually not a multidisciplinary team available to develop CALL resources, there are fewer financial resources and often not many available experts to contribute to the design and development process.

ICALL (Intelligent CALL) is a branch of CALL that includes the use of NLP resources in the design and development of CALL resources (Helft and Schulz, 2007). Many LCTLs are also Lesser Resourced Languages (LRLs) and there is often a lack of suitable, good quality NLP resources for LCTL CALL researchers to leverage. This is the case for most of the Celtic languages, although there are some high quality resources available for specific language and functions. For example, in the case of Irish, there is a Finite State Morphological Analyser (Ui Dhonnachada, 2002) and a parser (Lynn, 2016) that are of high quality and available for CALL resources to use. Mobile Assisted Language Learning (MALL) is of growing interest within the CALL community in recent years ((Holden & Sykes, 2011; Kukulska-Hulme, 2009; Kukulska-Hulme, 2012; Stockwell, 2012)) and there are many MALL apps being developed, particularly for the MCTLs.

Irish is a compulsory subject in Irish primary and secondary schools, although some students can get an exemption from studying the language. Reasons for exemptions include having a learning difficulty (e.g. dyslexia) or if the student came to Ireland after a certain age. In Irish primary schools, teachers are generalists and teach all subjects to their students, including Irish. At second level, teachers are specialists and will have four years of undergraduate study in their subject and two years postgraduate study in education. There are several issues to consider in relation to Irish language teaching. Most teachers, both at primary and secondary level, are not native speakers of the language. Primary teachers in particular have many subjects to cover and Irish is only one of them, so the level of ability in Irish can vary widely from one teacher to another. Some primary teachers are passionate about Irish, while others less so. Some teachers may lack confidence in their Irish language ability and this can have an impact on their teaching of the language. At second level, there is currently a shortage of Irish language teachers and it is hard from schools to find qualified teachers.

Language pedagogy is a specific branch of pedagogy. It is different from studying a subject like biology or history and it is important that teachers have knowledge of language teaching in order to help their students learn more efficiently, effectively and enjoyably. Learning a language does not just involve the four basic skills (reading, writing, listening and speaking), but involves cultural awareness and pragmatics, learning new sounds, having the courage to make mistakes and learn from them and sometimes thinking about things in a completely new way. In Ireland, students learn a Modern Foreign Language (MFL) (e.g. French, German or Spanish) in secondary school. MFL teachers study all aspects of language pedagogy. However, primary school teachers will only have limited exposure to language pedagogy as part of their pre-service teacher undergraduate study and will only have a limited knowledge of CALL. In some university departments there is a separate department for Irish and a different one for Modern Foreign Languages and this can sometimes mean that there may be a lack of cross-over knowledge in relation to language pedagogy and CALL. Also, there may be a focus on traditional aspects of language teaching with less space for more modern or innovative approaches. This in turn can result in less positive learning experiences for students learning Irish compared with a MFL. Their level of language attainment after 13 years of study is also quite low (Harris et al, 2006). Of course, there have been changes over the years and there are places where there is excellent and innovative teaching taking place, but there are still schools where there is plenty of room for improvement. The lack of teachers compounds this problem.

Irish has a paradoxical role in Ireland. Devitt et al. (2018) report on primary school children's attitude towards the language and their varying level disengagement with the language. Research shows that people value the language, they see it as part of Irish identify and recognise the cultural importance of the language (Darmody and Daly, 2015). However, when it comes to the classroom, sometimes they are less enthusiastic. Less importance may be attached to Irish language homework and some parents may prefer their child to study a 'useful' language like Spanish or Chinese. All Irish language speakers in Ireland also speak English and the lack of utilitarian value can impact perception of the language (Laoire, 2005). The paradoxical role of Irish can impact on teachers. They can feel the societal weigh of responsibility for teaching the language, yet feel little support from parents for the actual teaching of Irish. Negative attitudes towards the language can be demotivating for both teachers and students.

Irish App Development Challenges	
Challenge	**Comment**
CALL development is difficult	Difficult for any language, more so for Less Resourced Languages like Irish
Irish language teaching	Few teachers are L1 speakers, lack of confidence, not a focus for some
Irish language pedagogy	Pedagogy is improving but room for improvement
Paradoxical attitudes towards the language	Culturally valued, but less positive in reality

Table 1: List of Irish app development challenges

1.3 WordBricks

WordBricks is an interactive language learning app (Mozgovoy & Efimov, 2013). It was originally designed for adult learners (Japanese university students) of English. It is based on a visual learning paradigm, somewhat similar to the interface used in the visual programing language Scratch (Resnick et al., 2009; Wilson et al., 2013) and other work with blocks to illustrate grammar points Ebbels (2007). Each part of speech (POS) is given a different shape and colour (e.g. all verbs are blue and start with a straight edge). Learners can construct grammatically correct sentences by putting different parts of speech in the correct order in a sentence. In fact, learners can *only* construct grammatically sentences – the app will not allow them to put POS in the wrong place. The motivation behind the app was to enable learners to experiment with different sentences and play around with word order so that they could familiarise themselves with the structure of a language. When language students use a book to learn a language, they are often restricted to a limited number of example sentences or exercise sentences. They have to consult with their teacher if they want to check the correctness of sentences they construct themselves. This limits the freedom they have to work without teacher support and may restrict their motivation to try out new sentences for fear of making mistakes. The visual learning paradigm used by the app facilitates the pattern matching aspect of language learning, as the more sentences a student constructs, the more obvious the patterns become. Figure 1 shows an example of a sentence in English. The verb component 'saw' in blue and starting with a straight edge. It expects a subject that has a rounded side (in this case 'we') at the start of the sentence and it expects an object after the verb 'saw'. The object in this case is 'things' and it can be qualified by the words 'many' and 'interesting' as these are the correct shapes (parts of speech) that can precede the object 'things'. The full sentence of Figure 1 is 'We saw many interesting things in the museum' (although 'The interesting things saw we in the museum' would also be accepted).

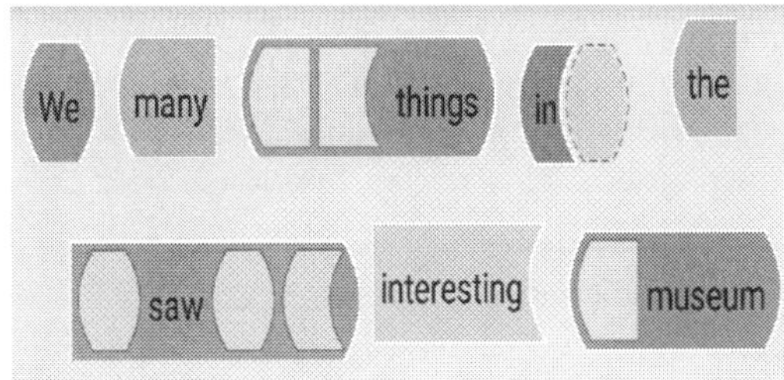

Figure 1: A sentence for the original WordBricks app for English

2 Approach

As with many Lesser Resourced Languages and LCTLs, Irish is under-served by CALL resources. It is not financially attractive for commercial entities to develop CALL resources for Irish. However, there are some good resources recently developed for learners. For example, Irish 101 on the FutureLearn platform is an online MOOC for learning Irish and culture (Irish101, n.d.). It is very successful and has had learners from all over the world studying Irish. Dalton and Devitt (2016) have developed a successful online detective game for primary school students. Hainey et al. (2016) provide an overview of game-based language learning resource at primary school level, including for language, and they note that many of them use commercial off the shelf (COTS) games. This is often not an option in the Irish context. As noted above, it is a challenge to develop CALL resources for Irish. Limited resources (financial, NLP and time) and lack of relevant experts demands a smart approach. A combination of refactoring, reuse and real-world focus were used to develop the Irish WordBricks app.

2.1 Refactoring

Refactoring is the process by which existing code is changed without changing its external behaviours (Fowler, 2018). Refactoring usually takes place when a code smell (lovely term) is detected (e.g. when something 'wrong' is noticed). This means that developers will review code that is unusually slow or could be improved (noticed by a 'code smell'). It can be done to improve maintainability and extensibility. Refactoring in this case took place in the context of making an existing app work in other contexts. WordBricks was initially developed as an app for Japanese university students of English (Park et al., 2016) and needed to be refactored to work for

Irish. The app had been successfully developed and used in a Japanese university, so the technology and the pedagogy had been tested and proved successful (Park et al., 2016). The aim was to refactor the English version of WordBricks so that it could be used to develop an app for Irish. The target user group, the setting and the devices used to run the app were all different. The original WordBricks was designed for adult learners to use outside of the classroom setting on a mobile phone. While it might be obvious, It is important to remember that education with adults (androgogy) is different to that with children (pedagogy) (Knowles, 1968). The Irish WordBricks app was aimed at young primary school learners, in a classroom setting on the teacher's laptop or a tablet. The refactoring process would involve keeping the same front-end functionality and User Interface (UI), but rework the back-end so that it was language independent.

2.2 Reuse

There were two elements that were reused in the development of the Irish WordBricks app. The first was the reuse of the original WordBricks app itself. The second element was the reuse of existing Irish NLP resources. These were the Finite State Morphological Analyser (FSMA) (Uí Dhonnchadha, 2002) and the Irish language parser (Lynn, 2016). The FSMA analyser is a high quality NLP resource for Irish and it produces Irish morpho-syntactic tags for an input sentence. The FSMA was used manually initially to check part of speech information when developing example sentences for the Irish WordBricks app. The Irish Parser produces treebank information for an input sentence. The idea was to use the knowledge in these resources to ensure the accuracy of the grammar constructions and words used in the Irish WordBricks app.

2.3 Real-World Focus

Many language learning apps and resources get built, tested in a controlled environment and never make it out to the wild (i.e. the real world). This may be because the app may not be sufficiently robust for external use or may need additional resources that are not available in the real world setting. Another reason that this sometimes happens is if the app is not curriculum-aligned. Curriculum-alignment is a key factor in CALL real-world usage for any language (Bax, 2003; Chambers and Bax (2006) and also for Irish

(Ward, 2007). The school curriculum, at both primary and secondary level, is packed. Teachers do not have spare teaching time to devote to additional, optional extras. Therefore, if an app is not curriculum-aligned teachers will be reluctant to use it. In order for an app to be actually useful for teachers and students, it must be designed with a real world focus from the start and be cognoscente of the actual deployment context and real world conditions prevailing in the learning environment. The Irish WordBricks app was designed using a user-centre design approach whereby the teachers were consulted at an early stage in the design process about what topics should be covered and how the app could be deployed in the classroom. They decided that possession, doing something, feeling something, location and asking questions where important topics to have in the app. The presumption was that the teacher would have already taught a topic before the students would use the app i.e. the app would be a tool rather than a tutor (Levy, 1997).

3   Methodology

The process of developing the Irish WordBricks (IWB) app took place in several phases. In the initial phase, the Irish CALL researcher worked in parallel with several primary school teachers and the WordBricks developers on possible grammatical constructs. The Irish CALL researcher and the teachers reviewed the Irish syllabus and current textbooks to decide on the topics to be covered and the vocabulary to be used in the app. The WordBrick developers worked on refactoring their app so that it would work for Irish as well as English. They then worked on incorporating the required grammatical information and vocabulary into the WordBricks infrastructure to create the first version of the Irish WordBricks app. In this Phase, the (Finite State Morphological Analyser (FSMA, Uí Dhonnchadha, 2002) was used (manually) to check the POS of each of the words in the example sentences and vocabulary lists. The information was passed to the WordBricks developers using an informal, ad-hoc structure and they incorporated it into their WordBricks engine (see Figure 2).

An iterative, agile approach was adopted, whereby one topic (grammatical construction) was implement and tested by the WordBricks developers, the CALL researcher and the teacher and checked for correctness before implementing

another topic. The target learner group (primary school children) also tested the app at an early stage to ensure that they could use it without any difficulties.

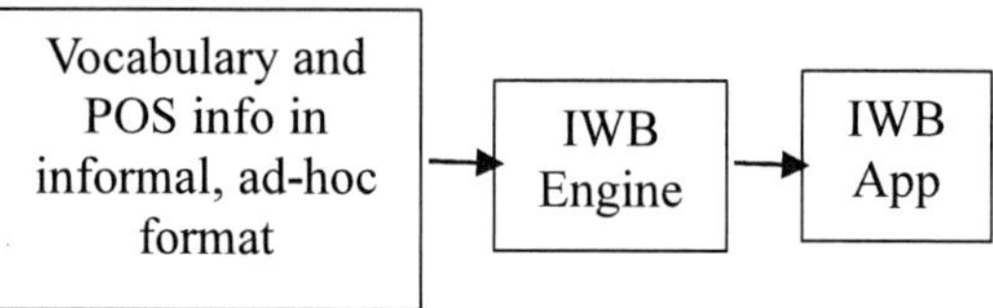

Figure 2: Phase 0 of Irish WordBrick development

Figure 3 shows the informal ad-hoc format used for the construction 'to have'. The WordBrick developers had no prior knowledge of Irish and it was necessary to explain both the vocabulary and part of speech information to them.

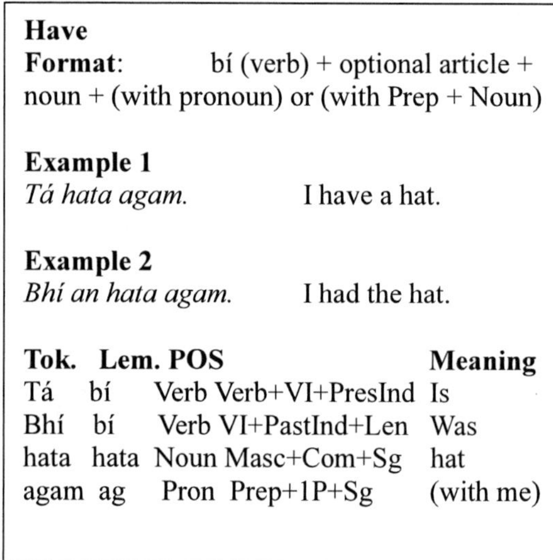

Have
Format: bí (verb) + optional article + noun + (with pronoun) or (with Prep + Noun)

Example 1
Tá hata agam.   I have a hat.

Example 2
Bhí an hata agam.   I had the hat.

Tok.	Lem.	POS		Meaning
Tá	bí	Verb	Verb+VI+PresInd	Is
Bhí	bí	Verb	VI+PastInd+Len	Was
hata	hata	Noun	Masc+Com+Sg	hat
agam	ag	Pron	Prep+1P+Sg	(with me)

Figure 3: Sample informal information for 'to have' construction

In Phase 1 of the IWB development, the individual example sentences where encoded in an XML file. All known words (with their POS information) were stored in the IWB app so that learners could construct their own new sentences as well as constructing the example sentences. This involved the Irish CALL researcher providing the WordBrick developers with the example sentences and the relevant vocabulary list specifying the POS of each word. This enabled the IWB app to be developed using the same black-box architecture as the original English WordBricks app (see Figure 4). While this was very beneficial, it was quite limiting as it was difficult to decide how best to structure the information and there was an associated turnaround time to enter new examples into the app.

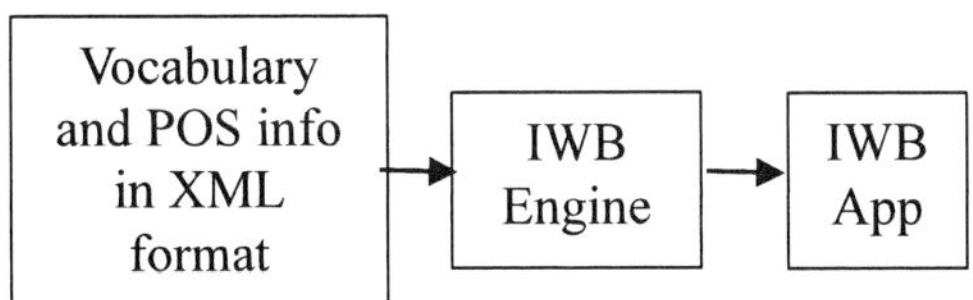

Figure 4: Phase 1 of the Irish WordBricks app

In Phase 2 of the IWB development, existing NLP resources for Irish were used to automate the process and enable learners to have access to a wider range of vocabulary. The Irish WordBricks app was developed on the basis of Uí Dhonnchadha's (2002) Finite State Morphological Analyser (FSMA) for Irish, Lynn's Irish parser (2015) and the Irish treebank (universal dependencies version, Lynn and Foster (2016). The user inputted sentence is passed to the FSMA for Irish (Uí Dhonnchadha, 2002). The FSMA produces Irish morpho-syntactic tags which are passed to the Irish parser (Lynn, 2016). The parser's output is then fed into the Irish WordBricks engine which takes maps the sentence into an XML structure. This XML data is passed into the IWB App where the learner can see the individual words and then construct a grammatically correct sentence. (see Figure 5). The Irish WordBricks app relies on the underlying NLP tools to handle ambiguity. One advantage of dealing with learners with a low level of language ability is that their choice of words is usually limited and they are unlikely to (be able to) construct complex sentences.

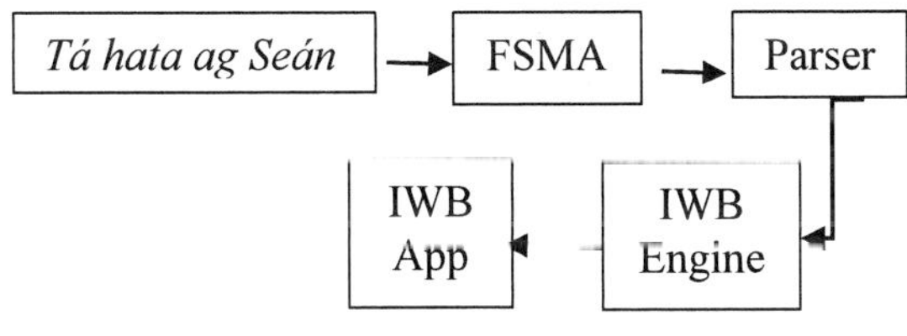

Figure 5: Phase 2 of the Irish WordBricks app using existing NLP resources

The topics covered in the IWB app include: to have something (*Tá hata agam.*), to do something (*Tá Seán ag rith*), feelings (*Tá áthas ar Liam*), location (*Tá leabhar ar an mbord*) and questions (*An raibh Áine ag ithe?*). Figure 6 shows the construction of simple sentence (*Tá hata agam –* I have a hat). If the word is the correct place, the learner will see the brick turning yellow and the word will clock into place.

Figure 6: Eample of a simple sentence in Irish WordBricks

Figure 7 shows an example of location (*Tá leabhar ar an mbord –* there is a book on the table).

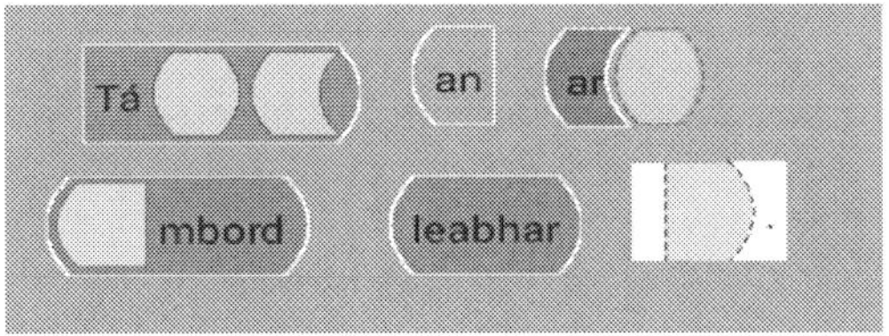

Figure 7: Example of location sentnce in Irish WorBricks

Figure 8 shows two sentences lined up together and illustrates how students can benefit from this visual learning approach (e.g. colours and shapes) to remember language and part of speech patterns in a sentence.

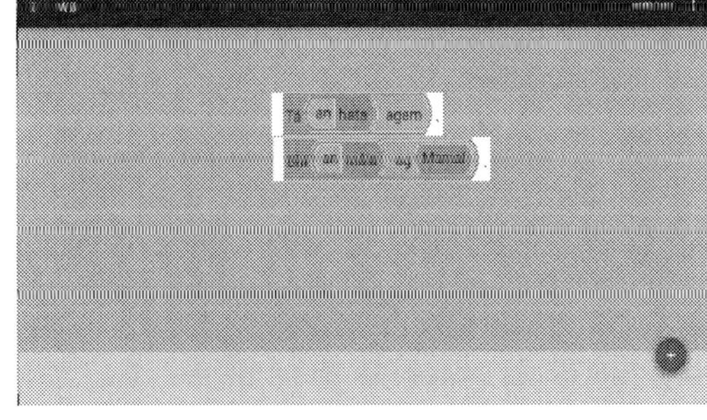

Figure 8: Example of two similar sentences lined up together in Irish WordBricks

Figure 9 shows how the app prevents a student from constructing a grammatically incorrect sentence. The student is trying to add the article '*na*' (definite plural) to a singular noun (*hata* – hat) and app does not let the student place the word there.

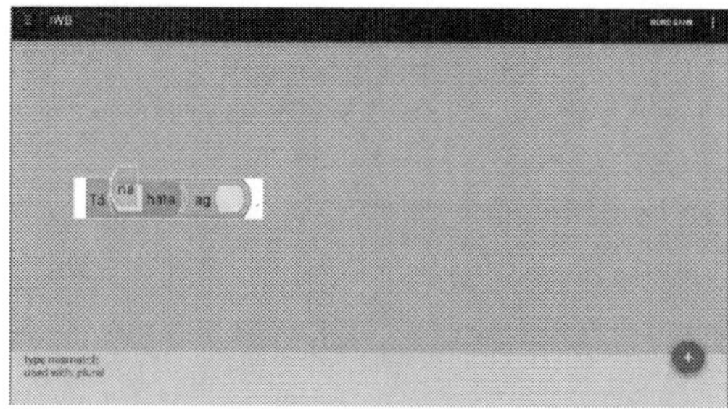

Figure 9: Example of Irish WordBricks preventing the construction of an incorrect sentence

4   Results

The app was initially tested with four adult learners of Irish. Their feedback was positive and they like the user interface and felt the app was easy to use. The app has been used by a variety of primary school learners (Purgina et al., 2017) over a period of three years (including this year). The app has been used by second class students (7-8 years old), third class students (8-9 years old) and fifth class students (10-11 years old). The app was used by three 3rd year classes (n=72) and two 5th year classes (n=44) in Year 1, three 2nd year classes (n=72) and two 5th year classes (n=52) in Year 2 and three 5th year classes (n=75) in Year 3. There were two primary schools involved – one all-boys and one all-girls. Three teachers were involved in the consultations about the content of the app.

The IWB app has been used in a variety of ways. Initially it was used in a whole class setting. This involved the teacher showing the students a particular construct (e.g. to have *Tá hata agam* – I have a hat). This involved putting the IWB on a laptop and using an android emulator to run the app and show it to the class via a data projector. The teacher would then ask some students to come up and construct the example sentences in front of the class. Then several students were chosen to construct their own sentences for the class. This approach worked reasonably well but more students wanted to use the app than time permitted. However, this was the only possible way of using the app as there were no computers or tables in the school for student use.

In the second year, students were given tablets to run the IWB app. Initially, they use the tablets in pairs but then they were given individual tablets to work with. This had the advantage of enabling students to work at their own pace. This is very important in a subject like Irish where there is a wide range of ability in each class. One slight disadvantage with this approach, is that students try to get the example sentences done as quickly as possible so they can construct their own sentences. Sometimes they try to set up loads of words and they can lose focus on the pedagogical aspects of the app.

In the third year (this current year), the deployment of the app is more structured. The teacher revises a particular construct with the students and asks them to write their own sentences on paper. The students can use the app to do the example sentences and then they can input their own sentences. This structured approach appears to be working well. In the first version of the app, the vocabulary was fixed and was based on the words that the students had studied with their teacher. In the second version of the app, the students have the facility to enter their own words.

Feedback from the students and teachers to date has been very positive. In the Irish language learning context, qualitative research is very important (Ward, 2018). The students find the app easy to use, they think it helped them to learn Irish, and most importantly, they enjoyed using the app (*"Really good, fun and easy to use"*). The students had many suggestions for future improvements. For example, they would like it to be more gamified (*"Maybe a challenge mode to test you"*), *"To challenge people online and get points for longer sentences"*, they would like translations (*"Every Irish word & English subtitles"*) and they would like more words (*"Add new verbs and different names"*). Some students wanted to know when they could download the app (*"Great help, can't wait until it's on the app store :-)"*) which is encouraging. One student had a great insight into the app *"I love the method it uses to create sentences. It's a bit like a puzzle in a way. I also adore the trial and error style"*. The teachers also had positive feedback. They were happy with the topics covered and were glad to see the level of interaction and engagement of the students with the app. Usually, their Irish lessons do not generate the same buzz in the classroom.

5   Discussion

It would not have been possible for the CALL

developer to develop the Irish WordBricks app from scratch in a reasonable timeframe. The fact that the original WordBricks app could be refactored to produce the Irish WordBricks app meant that learners could start using the app in a period of months rather than years. WordBricks has already been tried and tested with real users and had the WordBricks team demonstrated that it was a useful and viable app for learners. This gave confidence to the Irish WordBricks team that the aim of developing a useful, enjoyable app for Irish language learners was feasible rather than a pipedream.

It was very important that real learners used the app in their real world setting. The IWB app was curriculum-aligned right from the start and teachers were consulted throughout the design and development process. Learners were asked for their feedback and each version of the IWB app has included improvements based on their feedback. For example, students wanted to be able to save their sentences and this is now possible. Students wanted to be able to type in their own words and they can now do this.

From a technical perspective, the new version of the Irish WordBricks app allows for greater flexibility and demonstrates the power and potential of reusing existing NLP resources in the development of CALL resources for Irish. It would not have been possible to develop such a resource in a relatively short timeframe from scratch and it would have required technical and linguistic knowledge of Irish that only a very few people possess. Existing resources from Irish NLP researchers (Uí Dhonnchadha 2002, 2009; Lynn, 2016; Lynn and Foster, 2016) were invaluable in this regard.

6   Conclusion

Irish, like the other Celtic languages, would benefit from having more resources available for language learners. However, it is difficult to build robust, grammatically accurate, enjoyable resources for students. The IWB app works due to a variety of factors. The motivation behind the development of the app was strong – teachers, students and the CALL researcher knew that there was a real need for such an app. There was a multidisciplinary team involved in its development including teachers, students, CALL researchers, education design specialists and app developers. The concept and reality of the app had been proven in another domain. The IWB team was aware of, and consistently conscious of the real world deployment context of the app. An important aspect to be emphasized is that the system has been used by a variety of students ranging in age from 7 to 11 years and the final product is enjoyable for students and teachers also. The design and development of the IWB app demonstrates the power of refactoring, reuse and keeping it real.

References

Bax, S. (2003). CALL—past, present and future. *System, 31*(1), 13-28.

Chambers, A., & Bax, S. (2006). Making CALL work: Towards normalisation. *System, 34*(4), 465-479.

Dalton, G., & Devitt, A. (2016). Gaeilge Gaming: Assessing how games can help children to learn Irish. *International Journal of Game-Based Learning (IJGBL), 6*(4), 22-38.

Darmody, M., & Daly, T. (2015). *Attitudes towards the Irish Language on the Island of Ireland*.

Devitt, A., Condon, J., Dalton, G., O'Connell, J., & Ní Dhuinn, M. (2018). An maith leat an Ghaeilge? An analysis of variation in primary pupil attitudes to Irish in the growing up in Ireland study. *International Journal of Bilingual Education and Bilingualism, 21*(1), 105-117.

Dörnyei, Z., & Ushioda, E. (2013). *Teaching and researching: Motivation*. Routledge.

Duolingo (n.d.) Available at: https://www.duolingo.com/

Ebbels, S. (2007) Teaching grammar to school-aged children with specific language impairment using shape coding. *Child Language Teaching and Therapy 23* (1), 67–93.

Fowler, M. (2018). *Refactoring: improving the design of existing code*. Addison-Wesley Professional.

Hainey, T., Connolly, T. M., Boyle, E. A., Wilson, A., & Razak, A. (2016). A systematic literature review of games-based learning empirical evidence in primary education. *Computers & Education, 102*, 202-223.

Harris, J., Forde, P., Archer, P., & Nic Fhearaile, S. O Gorman, M.(2006). *Irish in primary school: Long-term national trends in achievement*.

Heift, T., & Schulze, M. (2007). *Errors and intelligence in computer-assisted language learning: Parsers and pedagogues*. Routledge.

Holden, C. L., & Sykes, J. M. (2011). Leveraging mobile games for place-based language learning. *International Journal of Game-Based Learning (IJGBL)*, *1*(2), 1-18.

Irish 101, n.d. Irish 101: An introduction to Irish language and culture. Available at: https://www.futurelearn.com/courses/irish-language

Kukulska-Hulme, A. (2009). Will mobile learning change language learning?. *ReCALL*, *21*(2), 157-165.

Kukulska-Hulme, A. (2012). Mobile-Assisted language learning. *The encyclopedia of applied linguistics*.

Laoire, M. Ó. (2005). The language planning situation in Ireland. *Current Issues in Language Planning*, *6*(3), 251-314.

Levy, M. (1997). *Computer-assisted language learning: Context and conceptualization*. Oxford University Press.

Levy, M., & Stockwell, G. (2013). *CALL dimensions: Options and issues in computer-assisted language learning*. Routledge.

Lynn, T., (2016). Irish Dependency Treebanking and Parsing. PhD Thesis.

Lynn, T., & Foster, J. (2016). Universal dependencies for Irish. In *Celtic Language Technology Workshop* (pp. 79-92).

Mozgovoy, M. & Efimov, R. (2013) WordBricks: a virtual language lab inspired by Scratch environment and dependency grammars. *Human-centric Computing and Information Sciences 3* (1), 1–9.

Nacke, L. E., & Deterding, C. S. (2017). The maturing of gamification research. *Computers in Human Behaviour*, 450-454.

Park, M., Purgina, M., & Mozgovoy, M. (2016). Learning English Grammar with WordBricks: Classroom Experience. In *Proceedings of the 2016 IEEE International Conference on Teaching and Learning in Education*.

Purgina, M., Mozgovoy, M., & Ward, M. (2017). MALL with WordBricks–building correct sentences brick by brick. *CALL in a climate of change: adapting to turbulent global conditions–short papers from EUROCALL 2017*, 254.

Reinhardt, J., & Sykes, J. (2014). Special issue commentary: Digital game and play activity in L2 teaching and learning. *Language Learning & Technology*, *18*(2), 2-8.

Resnick, M., Maloney, J., Monroy-Hernández, A., Rusk, N., Eastmond, E., Brennan, K., & Kafai, Y. (2009). Scratch: programming for all. *Communications of the ACM*, *52*(11), 60-67.

Stockwell, G. (2012). Mobile-assisted language learning. *Contemporary computer-assisted language learning*, *16*(3), 24-31.

Uí Dhonnchadha, E. (2002). *An analyser and generator for Irish inflectional morphology using finite-state transducers* (Doctoral dissertation, Dublin City University).

Uí Dhonnchadha, E. (2009). *Part-of-speech tagging and partial parsing for Irish using finite-state transducers and constraint grammar* (Doctoral dissertation, Dublin City University).

Ushioda, E. (Ed.). (2013). *International perspectives on motivation: Language learning and professional challenges*. Springer.

Ward, M. (2007). *The integration of CL resources in CALL for Irish in the primary school context* (Doctoral dissertation, Dublin City University).

Ward, M. (2018). Qualitative research in less commonly taught and endangered language CALL.

Wilson, A., Hainey, T., & Connolly, T. M. (2013). Using Scratch with primary school children: an evaluation of games constructed to gauge understanding of programming concepts. *International Journal of Game-Based Learning (IJGBL)*, *3*(1), 93-109.

Author Index